C000063862

QUIRKY CAREERS & OFFBEAT OCCUPATIONS OF THE PAST, PRESENT, AND FUTURE

EXPLORING WEIRD, WACKY, AND INTERESTING JOBS YOU NEVER KNEW EXISTED

MARIANNE JENNINGS

Stay Curious + Enjoy!
♡ MJ

KNOWLEDGE NUGGET BOOKS

CONTENTS

Quirky Careers & Offbeat Occupations of the Past, Present, and Future:

Exploring Weird, Wacky, and Interesting Jobs You Never Knew Existed

Cover design: Asya Blue

Editor: Joe Levit

Fact-checker: Hank Musolf

Library of Congress Control Number: 2023920461

ISBN: 979-8-9884402-2-2 (paperback)

ISBN: 979-8-9884402-3-9 (ebook)

Disclaimer: This book contains strange and unusual jobs you never knew existed, and once you know about them, you can't un-know them.

HOW TO READ THIS BOOK

This book is divided by topics, with links to jump to wherever you'd like.

There is no need to read this book cover to cover.

Just pick a subject that seems interesting and dig right in.

Please note: the salaries listed within are in US dollars.

To find out what you and your friends have learned, you'll find a fun, short quiz with answers in the back.

INTRODUCTION

Once upon a time, at the tender age of 14, I found myself milking cows in a quaint dairy down the lane. Little did I know, this was only the beginning of a whirlwind adventure through a whopping 26 colorful jobs! From maintaining hearses in a funeral home to plugging in lights on a board that ended up at the New York Stock Exchange, I even spent some time as a cookie-baking dental assistant – talk about an eclectic résumé!

This journey ignited a curiosity to delve into the nooks and crannies of the working world. And so, my friends, this book was born! A collection of peculiar, quirky, and lesser-known professions—some lost to time, others still thriving, and a few peeking around the corner.

Now, this isn't your average career guide, but rather a lighthearted and enjoyable read filled with fascinating facts about all sorts of jobs. So, whether you're on the hunt for a one-of-a-kind career or simply crave intriguing tidbits, this book has got you covered.

If you've stumbled upon a unique job that deserves a mention, don't hesitate to reach out—it might just land itself in a future edition!

So, grab a comfy chair, sit back and relax while you join me in exploring the fascinating, oft-overlooked realm of unconventional jobs. Prepare to be both entertained and enlightened.

Happy reading!

ECCENTRIC AND UNEXPECTED JOBS IN TRAVEL AND HOSPITALITY

If you love to travel and enjoy the hospitality industry, you'll be fascinated to learn about the unconventional jobs available in these fields. From sleeping in luxurious hotels as a bed tester to working as a butler on the beach, the opportunities are endless.

In this chapter, we'll explore the unique jobs that make traveling more enjoyable, and provide an unforgettable experience for guests. So buckle up for a wild ride as we uncover the eccentric and unexpected jobs in travel and hospitality.

LUXURY HOUSE SITTER 🏠👀🗝️💰😎

A luxury house sitter is hired to take care of wealthy people's homes while they're away on vacation.

Fun Fact: In some cases, luxury house sitters are also responsible for taking care of the homeowners' pets, plants—and even their yachts!

Salary: Around $80,000 per year.

CRUISE SHIP ENTERTAINER

Entertainers on cruise ships perform shows and other activities for passengers.

Fun Fact: Some cruise ship entertainment companies require their performers to be capable of walking on stilts, juggling, or performing other circus tricks.

Salary: $24,000 to $120,000 per year.

SLEEP CONCIERGE

A hotel employee who specializes in providing guests with the perfect sleep experience, including pillow and mattress selection, bedtime snacks, and relaxing music.

Fun Fact: The Benjamin Hotel in New York City is known for having a sleep concierge.

Salary: $40,000 to $60,000 per year.

BEACH BUTLER

Beach resorts often employ beach butlers to cater to guests' needs while they soak up the sun. From providing drinks and snacks to setting up umbrellas and chairs, beach butlers are there to make sure guests have a relaxing and enjoyable time. Some beach butlers may also offer additional services, such as sunscreen application, beachside massages or surf lessons.

Fun Fact: The world's most expensive beach butler service is offered at the Burj Al Arab hotel in Dubai, and includes private beach access, personal butlers assigned to each guest, and luxurious amenities such as inflatable toys, water sport equipment and massages.

Salary: The salary for a beach butler varies depending on the location and the employer. In the United States, the average hourly wage is between $12 to $20, with tips potentially increasing earnings. Based on the hourly wage of $12 to $20, a full-time beach butler could earn an annual salary of approximately $24,960 to $41,600 if they work 40 hours per week for 52 weeks.

HOT AIR BALLOON PILOT 🎈 ✈️ 💂

Photo by Pesce Huang on Unsplash

Hot air balloon pilots take passengers on scenic rides through the air, wherever the wind takes them.

Fun Fact: The first recorded hot air balloon flight took place in France in 1783 and lasted 25 minutes.

Salary: $30,000 to $60,000 per year.

HOSPITALITY EMOJI CREATOR

Some hotels and resorts have begun using custom-made emojis to communicate with guests via text message and social media.

Fun fact: The world's first emoji-themed hotel opened in Tokyo, Japan in 2015.

Salary: $75,000 per year.

VOLCANO TOUR GUIDE

A person who leads tours of active or dormant volcanoes, providing information about the geology, history, and culture of the surrounding area.

Fun Fact: Hawaii Volcanoes National Park in the United States is a popular destination for volcano tours.

Salary: $30,000 to $50,000 per year.

2

NATURE'S QUIRKY CAREERS

For many of us, spending time in nature is a peaceful and restorative experience. But did you know that there are people who get paid to work outside, surrounded by the beauty of nature?

In this chapter, we'll explore the unconventional and often-overlooked jobs that allow people to connect with nature while earning a living. From wildlife rehabilitators who nurse injured animals back to health to treehouse builders who craft unique, sustainable homes in the treetops, these jobs require a love of the outdoors and a willingness to work in challenging environments.

Let's explore the fascinating and quirky jobs that allow people to spend their days in the great outdoors!

WILDLIFE CROSSING GUARD 🦌🔴👨🔋🌳🚗

Wildlife bridge that allows animals to safely cross busy roads. Photo by bbsferrari via depositphotos.com

Wildlife crossing guards help protect animals by helping them safely cross roads, particularly in areas where wildlife crossings are common. They may also collect data on the types and numbers of animals crossing, and help maintain wildlife corridors.

Fun Fact: Some countries have built special wildlife bridges and tunnels to reduce the risk of road accidents involving wildlife, resulting in safer passage for animals and drivers alike.

Salary: $40,000 per year.

MUSHROOM FARMER 🍄🔪👨‍🌾🚜

Mushroom farmers grow and harvest various species of mushrooms for commercial purposes. There are over 10,000 known mushroom species, but only a fraction of these are cultivated for consumption. Mushroom farmers must have extensive knowledge about which types are safe to eat and which are not.

Fun Fact: In the late 19th and early 20th centuries, there was a sort of "gold rush" in the U.S. for mushroom farming, especially in Pennsylvania, which remains a significant producer of mushrooms in the country.

Salary: $30,000 to $70,000 per year.

ICEBERG MOVER

An iceberg mover's primary duty is to prevent massive chunks of ice from colliding with oil rigs, ships, or coastal areas. They also work on projects to move icebergs to areas where they could serve as a source of freshwater.

Iceberg movers use techniques like towing with ships, utilizing water cannons to erode one side, spraying the surface with seawater to influence melting, and pumping warm subsurface water to alter the iceberg's trajectory. Moving an iceberg can take days to weeks, depending on its size and the distance it needs to be relocated.

Fun Fact: Iceberg movers have also been called "iceberg cowboys," "iceberg wranglers," and "bergmen."

Salary: $50,000 to $100,000 per year.

DID YOU KNOW?

Did you know that since the Titanic sinking in 1912, there has been an organization dedicated to keeping ships safe from icebergs? It's called the International Ice Patrol! This group uses planes and satellites to track icebergs in the North Atlantic

Ocean, and they warn shipping companies about any potential hazards.

During iceberg season from February to July, they provide daily iceberg warnings. The United States Coast Guard operates the organization, with support from international partners. Thanks to their efforts, the International Ice Patrol has prevented many accidents and saved countless lives over the past century.

SEAWEED HARVESTER

Harvesting seaweed by hand at low tide in Jambiani, a village in Unguja, Tanzania. Photo by Yann Macherez, CC BY-SA 4.0, via Wikimedia Commons

Seaweed harvesters collect and process various species of seaweed for food, cosmetics, and other products. Not all seaweeds are the same. Harvesters might be looking for dulse, kelp, nori, or carrageen, each of which has its unique appearance, habitat, and culinary or industrial use.

Fun fact: Seaweed has been used as a food source for centuries in various cultures around the world.

Salary: $20,000 to $50,000 per year.

FIRE LOOKOUT 🔥 🌲 •• 🌲 🔽

Fire Lookout Tower in the Great Smokey Mountains in the USA. Photo by Kirk Thornton on Unsplash

Fire lookouts are the eyes in the sky for forests! They chill out in cool towers, keeping a sharp eye on the landscape for any sign of smoke or fire. These nature-loving guardians are super important for spotting wildfires early and helping to keep our forests safe.

Fun Fact: Did you know that some famous authors like Jack Kerouac and Edward Abbey worked as fire lookouts? They found inspiration in their solitary lookout towers, surrounded by breathtaking nature. Talk about a room with a view!

Salary: $30,000 to $60,000 per year.

STORM CHASER

Storm chasers are the daredevils of the weather world! They chase down tornadoes, hurricanes, and epic thunderstorms to study them, snap cool pics, or just feel the thrill. Some storm chasers even help science by capturing important and insightful data on these wild weather events.

Fun Fact: Some experienced storm chasers offer guided tours for thrill-seekers and weather enthusiasts who want a taste of the action. These tours provide a unique, hands-on experience of chasing storms, while the expert guides help ensure safety and teach about severe weather.

Salary: Hobbyist chasers might not make much, while pros can rake in $30,000 to $60,000 per year.

VOLCANOLOGIST

A volcanologist is a scientist who studies volcanoes and volcanic activity. They gather data and study the processes that occur within and around volcanoes.

Some volcanologists specialize in volcanoes on other planets and moons and are called space volcanologists. Did you know the largest volcano in our solar system, Olympus Mons, is on Mars, and some moons like Io of Jupiter, have very active volcanoes?

Fun Fact: There are over 1,500 potentially active volcanoes in the world, and around 50-70 of them erupt each year.

Salary: $60,000 to $100,000 per year.

CLOUD SEEDER

A cloud seeder is someone who uses chemicals or other methods to modify the weather by inducing rainfall or snowfall. It requires a lot of knowledge of meteorology and weather patterns. Cloud seeders often work from aircraft, flying into clouds to release the seeding agents.

Fun Fact: The first successful cloud seeding experiment was conducted in 1946 by American chemist and meteorologist, Vincent Schaefer.

Salary: $40,000 to $80,000 per year.

PROFESSIONAL TREEHOUSE BUILDER

Treehouse builders often work on custom projects for clients who want a unique and sustainable living space among the trees. They may also design and build treehouses for commercial use, such as for hotels or resorts.

Fun Fact: The Guinness World Record for the largest treehouse was set in 2013 by a team of treehouse builders in

Tennessee, with a structure that measured over 97 feet tall and included 11 levels!

Salary: Based on the hourly wage of $20 to $30, a full-time treehouse builder could earn an annual salary of approximately $41,600 to $62,400 if they work 40 hours per week for 52 weeks.

3

CREATURE CAREERS: FROM FURRY TO FEATHERY

For all the animal lovers out there, we're about to embark on a thrilling journey into the world of peculiar and captivating careers that revolve around our furry and feathery friends. From professional dog surf instructors who help pups ride the waves, to the brave souls who clean shark tanks, these jobs are a testament to the unique bond between humans and animals.

We'll also explore the roles of wildlife rehabilitators, snake milkers, and even animal psychologists, showcasing the diverse ways people dedicate their lives to understanding, caring for, and working alongside the animal kingdom.

Get ready to unleash your inner animal enthusiast as we delve into the fascinating realm of odd and interesting animal-related jobs!

ANIMAL YOGA INSTRUCTOR 💀🐐🧘

Goat yoga. Photo by Vivian Cai on Unsplash

Animal yoga instructors teach yoga classes that incorporate animals, typically domesticated pets like dogs, cats, or even goats.

Fun Fact: Goat yoga started as a social media trend and is now a popular way to practice yoga while connecting with animals.

Salary: $30,000 to $60,000 per year.

DOG SURFING INSTRUCTOR 💀🏄🐕🏖️

Dog surfing instructors may work for a surf school or may operate their own business. They teach dogs and their owners how to surf together.

Fun Fact: Dog surfing competitions are held worldwide, with proceeds often going to animal charities.

Salary: $25,000 to $50,000 per year.

ANIMAL COLORIST 🐾 🐼 🐶

Animal colorists are groomers or stylists who specialize in using pet-safe dyes and coloring techniques to create unique and artistic designs on animals, typically dogs. Their services are often requested for special events, competitions, or just for fun by pet owners who want to give their pets a distinctive and creative look.

Creative grooming competitions showcase the most elaborate and artistic pet dye jobs. Animal colorists can create a wide range of artistic designs, from simple patterns and color accents to more elaborate and detailed artwork that may resemble airbrushed tattoos or even full-body paint.

Fun Fact: One of the most expensive animal coloring jobs at $2,000, was for a dog named Bentley who was colored pink for a breast cancer research charity.

Salary: $25,000 to $50,000 per year.

WORM PICKER 🐛 🐒 🪱

Worm pickers are the unsung heroes of the fishing and composting worlds! These night crawlers (the humans, not the worms) venture out under the cover of darkness to scoop up earthworms that wiggle their way to the surface. They then sell their wriggly finds to grateful fishermen or gardeners.

Fun Fact: Did you know that earthworms breathe through their skin? That's why they come to the surface when it rains – to avoid drowning. Worm pickers take advantage of this to snatch them up more easily. It's like a worm dance party every time it rains!

Salary: $20,000 to $30,000 per year. Pickers are usually paid based on the number of worms they collect, with rates around $0.02 to $0.05 per worm. A skilled worm picker could make $50 to $100 a night.

BUTTERFLY FARMER 🦋🌼🌱🐛

Butterfly farmers are the magical creatures who breed and raise butterflies for release into the wild, during weddings, or at other special events. They get to work with some of the most colorful and delicate creatures in the world, creating an enchanting experience for people everywhere.

Fun Fact: Did you know that butterflies taste with their feet? Yup, those little taste buds on their toes help them identify plants and find nectar.

Salary: $25,000 to $60,000 per year.

POOCH PAMPERERS 🐼🦮🐕🐩🐰

Pooch pamperers are the ultimate doggie spa experts! They spoil our furry friends with luxury treatments like grooming, massages, and even mani-pedis (paw-dicures?). Their job is to make sure our canine pals look and feel their absolute best, and let's be real, who doesn't love a fluffy, fresh-smelling dog? Pooch

Pamperers often provide their services to wealthy clients who want their dogs to be pampered like royalty.

Fun fact: Some high-end pooch pamperers offer fancy services like mud baths, blueberry facials, and aromatherapy for dogs. Yup, dogs can get the royal treatment too, and they totally deserve it!

Salary: On average, pooch pamperers can earn anywhere from $25,000 to $50,000 per year, with some earning even more in upscale areas or by offering premium services.

PET DETECTIVES 🐾🔍🕵️🕵️🐾

A pet detective is like the Sherlock Holmes of the animal world! These super sleuths track down lost or stolen pets using their keen investigative skills and a little high-tech gadgetry. Some even use search dogs trained specifically to sniff out lost animals, like cats or other dogs! They're on a mission to reunite families with their beloved furry friends.

Fun Fact: Remember Ace Ventura, the hilarious pet detective played by actor Jim Carrey? Well, real-life pet detectives might not be as wacky, but they're just as dedicated to cracking the case of missing pets.

Salary: Pet detectives often work as private investigators on a freelance basis, so their salaries can vary quite a bit. They might charge hourly rates or flat fees per case, ranging from $50 to $150 per hour plus expenses. A rough estimate would be $30,000 to $75,000 per year depending on their experience and reputation.

SHARK TANK CLEANER

Shark tank cleaners are the fearless underwater janitors who keep aquariums spick and span for our toothy shark friends. These brave souls dive right into the action, scrubbing algae, cleaning filters, and making sure the tank is in fin-tastic shape for the sharks.

Fun fact: Some shark tank cleaners have a special bond with their shark buddies. They get to know the sharks' personalities and even give them names. These skilled cleaners can distinguish between different sharks just by looking at them, which is jaws-droppingly cool!

Salary: When it comes to the bucks, shark tank cleaners typically fall under the umbrella of commercial divers or aquarium staff. Their salaries can range from $30,000 to $50,000 per year.

BEE WRANGLER

Bee wranglers are the beekeeping pros who handle honeybees and other bees with ease. They keep these tiny pollinators healthy and happy, making sure they produce delicious honey and keep our environment buzzing. This job involves relocating and managing bee colonies. It's like being a bee whisperer!

Fun Fact: Did you know that honeybees can fly up to 15 miles per hour and beat their wings 200 times per second?

Salary: $30,000 to $60,000 or more per year.

SLOTH KEEPER 🦥🤠

Sloth and its keeper. Photo by Denys Gromov via Pexels.com

Sloth keepers are the ultimate chill masters! These lucky caretakers get to hang out with the world's slowest mammals all day long, making sure they're happy, healthy, and as relaxed as can be. It's a pretty sweet gig, if you ask us!

Fun Fact: Did you know that sloths only poop once a week? Yup, you read that right—they save up all their business for one epic bathroom break.

Salary: $25,000 to $50,000 per year.

WHALE FECES RESEARCHER

Whale feces researchers are the brave souls who dive deep into the world of...well, whale poop! These scientists study the stinky stuff to learn more about the diets, health, and behavior of our ocean's gentle giants. It might sound gross, but whale poop is a goldmine of information!

Fun fact: Whale poop is actually super important for the ocean ecosystem. It helps fertilize plankton growth, which then pulls carbon dioxide from the atmosphere and produces oxygen.

Salary: Whale feces researchers fall under the broader category of marine biologists and their salaries can range from $40,000 to $80,000 or more per year.

ANIMAL FORENSIC SPECIALIST

Animal forensic specialists are the crime scene investigators of the animal world! These specialized vets and scientists use their skills to investigate animal-related crimes, like animal abuse or poaching. It's like CSI, but for animals!

Animal forensic specialists handle a wide range of cases, from investigating animal cruelty and abuse to identifying poached wildlife products and supporting prosecution efforts against wildlife traffickers.

Fun fact: Dr. Michael Blackwell was the first animal forensic specialist. He founded the American College of Veterinary Forensic Medicine in 1999. This organization currently has over 100 members from the United States and Canada.

Salary: $50,000 to $100,000 or more per year.

LLAMA THERAPIST

Llama therapists use the calming and adorable nature of llamas to help people feel better. These gentle and lovable creatures are used in therapy sessions to help reduce stress, anxiety, and depression. Llamas have been used for therapy since the 1990s.

Fun Fact: Did you know that llamas are used as pack animals and can carry up to 30% of their body weight on their backs?

Salary: $30,000 to $60,000 or more per year.

RODEO CLOWN

Rodeo clown (circled) at a rodeo in Tuscon, Arizona. Photo by Dulcey Lima on Unsplash

Rodeo clowns are the brave and wacky performers who entertain and distract bulls and other rodeo animals during competitions. They put their lives on the line to keep the animals and riders safe, all while making us laugh with their silly antics.

Fun Fact: While rodeo clowning can be a dangerous job, most professional rodeo clowns undergo extensive training to learn how to safely distract bulls and protect riders. They are professional athletes who undergo rigorous physical training to perform their job.

Salary: $30,000 to $100,000 or more per year.

FALCONER

Falconers are the bird-loving experts who train and work with birds of prey, like falcons and hawks. They use their skills to train these birds for hunting or for demonstrations, and work closely with these majestic creatures to help them reach their full potential.

Fun Fact: Did you know that peregrine falcons can dive at speeds of up to 200 miles per hour? That's as fast as Japanese Bullet Trains!

Salary: $30,000 to $80,000 or more per year.

CHICKEN SEXER

These professionals determine the sex of newly hatched chicks by examining their physical characteristics. They may work in hatcheries or in poultry processing plants.

Fun Fact: Determining the sex of chickens is a specialized skill that requires extensive training and experience.

Salary: $25,000 to $40,000 per year.

PENGUINOLOGIST

Penguinologists are the penguin experts who study everything about these adorable flightless birds! They get to hang out with penguins all day long, studying their behavior, habitat, and diet.

Fun Fact: Did you know that penguins have a gland above their eyes that filters out excess salt from the seawater they drink?

Salary: Penguinologists usually work in the field of marine biology or zoology. Salaries can range from $40,000 to $80,000 per year.

PET TRANSPORTER

Pet transporters are the road trip gurus of the animal world! These animal-loving drivers transport pets from one location to another, making sure they're comfortable, safe, and happy on the journey. Pet transporters don't just deal with cats and dogs; they may also transport small farm animals, and even exotic pets like reptiles and birds.

Fun Fact: Some pet transporters are members of professional organizations like the International Pet and Animal Transportation Association (IPATA), which sets standards and guidelines for the safe and humane transportation of pets.

Salary: $30,000 to $60,000 or more per year.

PANDA NANNY

Panda nannies are the lucky folks who get to work with the most adorable creatures on the planet—giant pandas! They take care of these fluffy bears, making sure they're well-fed, happy, and healthy.

Fun Fact: Did you know that baby pandas are born pink and hairless, and weigh only about 3 to 5 ounces? That's smaller than a can of soda!

Salary: $32,000 to $60,000 per year.

SNAKE MILKER

Venom of a cobra being extracted. Photo by yongkiet via Depositphotos.com

Snake milkers extract venom from snakes for medical research and the production of antivenom. They may work in zoos or research facilities. Some snake milking facilities also offer tours and allow visitors to watch the milking process. Snake venom is used in medical research to study the nervous system and to develop new painkillers.

Fun Fact: The venom from one king cobra can be used to produce enough antivenom to save 50 people.

Salary: $30,000 to $60,000 per year.

CRYPTOZOOLOGIST

A person who studies or investigates cryptids, which are animals or creatures whose existence has been suggested but not yet scientifically proven. Cryptozoology is considered a pseudoscience, as it relies on anecdotal evidence, folklore, and unverified sightings rather than empirical scientific methods.

Cryptozoologists investigate reports of mysterious creatures such as Bigfoot, the Loch Ness Monster, the Yeti, and the Chupacabra, among others. They often collect stories, eyewitness accounts, and any physical evidence such as footprints or photographs, in their attempts to prove the existence of these elusive creatures.

Fun Facts: The term "cryptozoology" was coined by zoologist Bernard Heuvelmans in the 1950s. It comes from the Greek words "kryptos," meaning hidden, and "zoology," the study of animals.

Salary: As cryptozoology is not a recognized scientific field and does not have a well-defined career path, salary is hard to estimate. Many cryptozoologists pursue their interests in cryptids as a hobby or side project rather than a full-time profession. Those who work in cryptozoology often do so independently or through small organizations dedicated to the study of mysterious creatures.

4

ROLL CREDITS... AND MEET THE MASTERS BEHIND THE MAGIC!

The dazzling world of arts and entertainment might be well-known for its shining stars, but there's a whole universe of unsung heroes working behind the scenes to make the magic happen.

In this chapter, join us on a fascinating journey to uncover the lesser-known but equally important jobs that contribute to the enchanting experiences we enjoy on stage, screen, and beyond. From wig masters who design fabulous hairpieces for stage and screen to the creative visionaries like makeup artists who transform ordinary spaces into extraordinary realms, these hidden talents are the secret ingredients that make the world of arts and entertainment truly mesmerizing. So, let's pull back the curtain and step into the thrilling backstage world where dreams come to life and inspiration takes center stage!

FOLEY ARTIST 🎬📽️🎞️🎧🎵

Foley artist with hands inside dress shoes walking on rocks. Photo via depositphotos.com

Foley artists are the sound wizards who work in the film and television industry. They use their skills to create and record sound effects, from footsteps to gunshots to explosions, and add them to movies and TV shows to make them more immersive and realistic.

One of the most challenging aspects of a Foley artist's job is syncing their live sound effects with the actions in the movie. It requires an impeccable sense of timing and often multiple takes to get just right.

The art of foley is named after Jack Foley, a pioneering sound effect artist who started in the film industry during the silent movie era and made significant contributions when films transitioned to sound.

Fun Fact: Did you know that the sound of lightsabers in the *Star Wars* movies was created by recording the hum of an old TV set and blending it with the sound of a film projector motor?

Salary: $30,000 to $100,000 per year.

PYROTECHNICIAN

Pyrotechnicians are the folks who work behind the scenes to create the explosions, fireworks, and other fire effects that you see in movies, TV shows, and live events. They use their knowledge of chemicals and physics to create stunning displays that awe and entertain audiences.

Fun Fact: Did you know that the biggest firework ever recorded was launched in Steamboat Springs, Colorado in the United States in 2020 and weighed over 2,800 pounds (1,270kg)? That's heavier than most cars!

Salary: $35,000 to $100,000 per year.

TITLE DESIGNER

Title designers, also known as motion graphic designers or title sequence designers, are professionals who create the opening titles, end credits, and other text elements for films, television shows, and video games.

Fun Fact: There are awards dedicated to recognizing excellence in title design, such as the Emmy Award for Outstanding Main Title Design and the SXSW Film Design Awards. Examples of films and TV shows that have won include *Game of*

Thrones (2011), *Westward* (2017) and *Into the Spider-Verse* (2019).

Salary: $45,000 to $100,000 per year.

PROP MAKER

Prop makers are the creative geniuses who design and build the props that you see on stage and screen. They use their skills in carpentry, sculpting, and painting to create everything from swords and guns to alien spaceships and magical wands.

Fun Fact: Did you know that the boulder from the opening scene of the movie *Indiana Jones and the Raiders of the Lost Ark* was actually made of fiberglass and weighed about 300 pounds?

Salary: $35,000 to $70,000 per year.

DIALECT COACH

Dialect coaches are the language experts who help actors and performers master different accents and dialects for movies, TV shows, and theater productions. They use their knowledge of linguistics and speech patterns to teach actors how to sound like they're from a different part of the world or even a different time period.

Fun Fact: Did you know that Meryl Streep hired a dialect coach to help her master the Polish accent for her role in the movie *Sophie's Choice*?

Salary: $40,000 to $100,000 per year.

DIALOGUE EDITORS

Dialogue editors are responsible for cleaning up and enhancing the audio recordings of actors' dialogue in movies and TV shows. They work closely with the sound department and the post-production team to ensure that the dialogue is clear, consistent, and matches the lip movements of the actors on screen.

Fun Fact: Did you know that dialogue editors sometimes have to work with audio recordings that were captured in less-than-ideal conditions, such as noisy or windy outdoor locations? They use a variety of techniques and software tools to clean up the audio and make it sound as seamless and natural as possible.

Salary: $40,000 to $100,000 per year.

COLORIST

Colorists are wizards of the movie and film industry, responsible for adding color to raw footage and creating a consistent look and feel for the final product. They work closely with directors, cinematographers, and editors to ensure that the color grading matches the desired tone and mood of the film.

Fun Fact: Did you know that colorists often have to work with footage that was shot under different lighting conditions and at different times of day? They use their expertise to balance out the colors and create a seamless visual experience for the audience.

Salary: $40,000 to $150,000 per year.

WIG MASTERS 🦱 👀 🎭 💆 💇

Wig makers or wig masters are the skilled artisans who design and create the wigs and hairpieces that you see on stage and screen. They use their knowledge of hair styling and wig-making techniques to create everything from historical hair-styles to fantastical wigs for characters in movies and TV shows.

Fun Fact: Did you know that it can take 40 hours or more to create one high-quality wig? High-quality wigs used in films and TV shows are often handmade, with wig makers meticulously knotting individual strands of hair onto a fine mesh cap to create a natural and realistic appearance.

Salary: $40,000 to $80,000 per year.

COSTUME PAINTER 🎨 💆 👗 🎭 👚

Costume painters are the skilled artisans who paint and dye costumes for movies, TV shows, and theater productions. They use their knowledge of color theory and textile properties to create unique and beautiful costumes that bring characters to life.

Costume painters use a variety of techniques including airbrushing, screen-printing, and hand-painting. Their work includes things like painting patterns onto fabrics, adding weathering effects and even adding metallic accents to costumes.

Fun Fact: In the *Lord of the Rings* Trilogy, costume painters played a huge part in creating visually stunning costumes for a large variety of characters. They created everything from the rugged looks of the Rohirrim to the elegant robes of the Elves. To make the costumes look worn and aged, costume painters used weathering techniques.

Salary: $35,000 to $70,000 per year.

MAKEUP ARTISTS

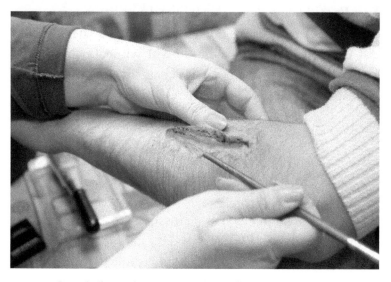

Special effects makeup artist creating artificial wound. Photo via depositphotos.com

Makeup artists are the magical people who use their skills to transform actors and models into characters with their makeup and hairstyling. They use their creativity and knowledge of makeup techniques to create everything from natural looks to fantastical makeup for movies and TV shows.

Creating realistic special effects makeup, like wounds or burns, often requires a deep understanding of human anatomy. Artists might study images from medical textbooks or work with forensic professionals to create the most authentic effects.

Fun Fact: When movies were primarily in black and white, makeup artists had to use colors that looked very odd in real life to achieve the desired contrast on black-and-white film. For example, green or blue lipsticks was used because they appeared the right shade of grey on screen.

Salary: $30,000 to $90,000 per year.

DIGITAL MAKEUP ARTISTS

Digital makeup artists are the talented professionals who use digital tools to enhance the appearance of actors in movies and TV shows. Digital makeup artists may be involved in a wide range of tasks, such as retouching and enhancing actors' appearances, creating realistic wounds or scars, transforming actors into otherworldly creatures, or even designing entirely new characters.

Fun Fact: Digital makeup artists have contributed to many high-profile films and television shows, such as *Game of Thrones, The Avengers*, and *The Curious Case of Benjamin Button*.

Salary: $50,000 to $150,000 per year.

SCRIPT RESEARCHER

These are the unsung heroes who do all the behind-the-scenes work to make sure that the script is accurate and factually correct. They may spend hours digging through archives, interviewing experts, and scouring the internet to make sure that every detail in the script is spot-on.

Fun Fact: Did you know that the iconic "I'll be back" line in the movie *The Terminator* was originally written as "I'll come back"? It was actually script researcher Sharon Boyle who suggested the change. Boyle thought "I'll come back" didn't have the same impact. Director James Cameron loved the suggestion, and the rest is history!

Salary: $50,000 to $70,000 per year.

SCRIPT SUPERVISORS

Script supervisors play a critical role in film and TV productions, helping to ensure that each shot is consistent with the script and the overall vision of the production. They work closely with the director and the production team to track changes to the script, monitor continuity, and ensure that actors deliver their lines correctly.

They make sure the actors are wearing the correct costumes, that the props are in the right place, that any special makeup looks the same in all of the shots, and that the scenes are shot in the correct order.

Script supervisors have to be incredibly detail-oriented and organized, as they are responsible for keeping track of every shot and take during filming.

Fun Fact: Margaret Booth was the first official script supervisor. She worked on films like *The Wizard of Oz*, *Funny Girl*, *The Way We Were* and *Annie*.

Salary: $40,000 to $100,000 per year.

DRONE LIGHT SHOW TECHNICIAN 🚁 💥

Drone firework technicians are the tech-savvy professionals who use drones to create stunning aerial displays for events like concerts, celebrations, and even sports games. They use their knowledge of drone technology and pyrotechnics to create dazzling light shows that can be choreographed to music.

Fun Fact: Did you know that some drone firework technicians are specially trained in creating drone light shows that can even create 3D images in the sky? For example, at King Charles III's Coronation Concert in 2023, a 3D butterfly, a swimming whale, a rabbit and other animals were a major part of the show.

Salary: $50,000 to $100,000 per year.

LASER LIGHT SHOW ARTISTS 💥🔥

Laser light show artists are the creative geniuses who use lasers to create spectacular light displays for concerts, festivals, and other events. They use their knowledge of laser technology and their artistic skills to create mesmerizing and visually stunning light shows that can include everything from colorful patterns to 3D projections. Often these laser shows are synced up with music.

Fun Fact: The world's largest laser show was seen by over 1 million people with over 1,000 lasers and was held in Beijing, China in 2018.

Salary: $40,000 to $100,000 or more per year.

BODY PAINTERS

Body painters are the artists who transform the human body into a canvas, using paint and other materials to create stunning works of art. They often work in the entertainment industry, creating bold and eye-catching designs for events, music videos, and photo shoots.

Fun Fact: Did you know that body painting has been around for thousands of years, with evidence of it dating back to ancient civilizations? From tribal ceremonies to modern-day art installations, the human body has long been a source of inspiration for painters and artists of all kinds.

Salary: $50,000 to $100,000 per year.

ICE SCULPTOR

Ice sculptors are the artists who use their creativity and carving skills to transform blocks of ice into stunning sculptures. They use a variety of tools, like chainsaws and chisels, to create intricate and detailed designs that can range from small, tabletop sculptures to massive ice installations.

Fun Fact: Did you know that some ice sculptors specialize in creating interactive ice installations, like ice slides or ice bars?

Salary: $30,000 to $80,000 per year.

ESCAPE ROOM DESIGNER

Escape room designers are the creative masterminds behind those thrilling and challenging interactive games where you and your friends have to solve puzzles and clues to escape a room. They come up with the concept, design the puzzles and obstacles, and create the immersive environment that brings the game to life.

Fun Fact: Did you know that the first escape room game was created in Japan in 2007? Since then, the trend has exploded, with thousands of escape rooms now in operation all over the world.

Salary: $30,000 to $60,000 per year.

THEME PARK RIDE DESIGNER

These are the creative minds behind the rides that make you scream, laugh, and hold on for dear life! They design everything from roller coasters to water slides, and work with engineers, animators, and special effects experts to create unforgettable experiences for theme park guests.

Fun Fact: Did you know that some theme park ride designers start out as roller coaster enthusiasts? That's right, some of the best ride designers are people who have spent their whole lives riding roller coasters and dreaming up their own designs. And when it comes to designing a new ride, they'll often test out their ideas by building scale models or even riding simulators to get a sense of what the ride will feel like.

Salary: $45,000 to $100,000+ per year.

MOTION CAPTURE ARTISTS

Have you ever seen a video game character move so smoothly that it almost looks real? That's the magic of motion capture, and motion capture artists are the magicians behind it all. These artists use special cameras and sensors to record the movements of actors or stunt performers and turn them into lifelike animations for movies, video games, and other media.

Fun Fact: Motion capture has been around for decades, but it's still evolving. Early motion capture techniques involved sticking sensors all over an actor's body, but now, some companies are experimenting with full-body suits that can capture even more subtle movements.

Salary: $35,000 to $80,000+ per year.

GAMEPLAY BALANCER

A gameplay balancer or game balancer helps make a game fair, fun, challenging, and an enjoyable experience. They use data and feedback to guide their decisions, but they also rely on intuition and experience to ensure the game feels right.

Fun Fact: Game balancing can be a difficult task, as each player has a unique skill level and playing style. Game balancers must take into account different levels of expertise and adjust the gameplay accordingly.

Salary: $50,000 to $100,000 per year.

LORE WRITER

Lore writers, also known as narrative designers or game writers, are responsible for creating the stories, characters, and worlds that make up the fictional universes of video games. They work closely with game designers and artists to ensure that the lore is consistent and immersive, and they often have to do extensive research on topics like history, mythology, and science fiction to create rich and believable narratives.

Fun Fact: The lore of a video game can often become just as important as the gameplay itself, with dedicated fans poring over every detail and developing their own theories and fan fiction. In fact, some video game lore has become so popular that it has spawned entire communities and even inspired its own merchandise and media.

Salary: $40,000 to $100,000+ per year.

GAME ECONOMISTS 💰🎮📊🧑‍💼🧑‍💼

Game Economists are responsible for designing and balancing the in-game economy of a video game. They use data analysis, mathematical models, and game design principles to create virtual economies that are fair, balanced, and engaging for players. They work closely with game designers, developers, and analysts to make the game enjoyable while making sure it makes money too.

Fun Fact: Game Economists are sometimes called "virtual economists" because they apply real-world economic principles to virtual worlds and economies.

Salary: $50,000 to $120,000 or more per year.

GAMEPLAY VIDEOGRAPHER 🎥🧑‍💼🧑‍💼🧑‍💼🎬

A gameplay videographer is responsible for recording footage of video games and creating video content for promotional and marketing purposes. They capture in-game footage and edit it to create videos that showcase the gameplay mechanics, story-lines, and overall gaming experience. They may also provide commentary on the game and help develop marketing strategies to promote the game to potential players.

Fun Fact: The first gameplay videos were created in the early 1980s and were often created by gamers themselves. They would use simple recording devices to capture their gameplay and then edit the footage together. These videos were often low-quality and grainy, but they helped popularize video games.

Salary: $45,000 to $65,000 per year.

JINGLE WRITER 🎶🎵🎤🎧🎬

Jingle writers are the creative folks who compose catchy tunes for ads, TV shows, and radio commercials. A great jingle writer knows how to write a short and sweet tune, usually around 30 seconds long, that still packs a punch. Jingle writers often work with singers, musicians, and sound engineers to bring their tunes to life.

Fun Fact: Sometimes, famous musicians are hired to create jingles, adding a little star power to the mix!

Salary: $30,000 to $100,000 per year.

5

WORKING WITH THE DEPARTED

While death is a natural part of life, what happens after we die remains one of the biggest mysteries in the universe. But did you know that there are many people out there whose jobs revolve around the afterlife?

From death midwives who help people transition peacefully to the next world, to ghost hunters who investigate paranormal activity, these jobs offer a unique perspective on what happens beyond the veil. We'll also dive into the fascinating work of forensic anthropologists, who examine bones to solve cold cases, and cemetery restorers who preserve our final resting places for future generations.

Come along for a ghostly ride as we uncover the strange and captivating jobs that exist in the world of the dead!

MORTUARY BEAUTICIAN 🪦 💇 👵 👨

These professionals apply makeup and style hair to make the deceased look more presentable for funerals.

Fun Fact: Mortuary beauticians often work closely with grieving families to create a personalized and meaningful final appearance for their loved ones.

Salary: $25,000 to $60,000 per year.

CADAVER DOG HANDLER 🐶 🐾 👮 🔍 💀

A volunteer from Bucks County Search and Rescue, and cadaver dog Tucker, search the wreckage of a Navy P-2V Neptune aircraft that crashed over Greenland in 1962.

A cadaver dog handler is a professional who works with specially trained dogs to locate human remains, including remains that have been buried or submerged in water. The dog handlers often work with law enforcement agencies and search and rescue teams to locate missing persons or victims of crimes.

Fun Fact: Cadaver dogs are trained to detect the scent of decomposition, which can remain present in the air for up to two years after a body has been removed.

Salary: $20,000 to $60,000 per year.

DEATH MIDWIFE

Death midwives, or end-of-life doulas, offer emotional, spiritual, and practical support to individuals and their families during the end-of-life process. They help with planning, advocacy, education, legacy work, and vigil and bereavement support.

Death midwives work closely with other professionals involved in end-of-life care, such as hospice staff, nurses, and doctors, to provide a holistic and collaborative approach to the dying process.

Fun Fact: The profession has ancient roots, with similar roles existing in many cultures throughout history.

Salary: $20,000 to $70,000 per year.

FUNERAL PLANNER

Funeral planners help families plan and coordinate funerals. They work with families to choose the type of funeral they want, select a funeral home and cemetery, and arrange for all of the necessary details, such as transportation, flowers, and music. Funeral planners can also help families to budget for the funeral and to apply for any financial assistance that may be available.

Fun Fact: There are also funeral planners who specialize in planning and arranging funerals for pets.

Salary: Salary varies widely depending on experience, location and the size of the funeral home, but average salary between $40,000 to $60,000 per year.

CEMETERY MANAGER 🪦 🏠 🌳 🧸 💀

These workers oversee maintaining cemetery grounds including tasks such as digging graves, setting headstones, and landscaping.

Fun Fact: Some famous people started their careers as cemetery groundskeepers, including the musician James Brown and actor Danny Glover.

Salary: $25,000 to $45,000 per year.

CEMETARY RESTORER 🪦 🔧 🧠 🔍 🧽

A cemetery restorer, or graveyard conservator, is a professional who preserves, maintains, and restores historic cemeteries. They repair tombstones, conserve monuments, manage landscaping, and occasionally research the site's history, ensuring the cemetery stays historically accurate and visitor-friendly.

Fun Fact: Cemetery restorers sometimes use a technique called "dowsing" or "divining" to locate unmarked graves. This method involves using a dowsing rod (often a Y- or L-shaped rod) to detect changes in the ground, such as differences in soil composition or the presence of a buried coffin.

Salary: $30,000 to $45,000 per year.

MEMORIAL TATTOO ARTIST

Memorial tattoo artists specialize in creating tattoos that commemorate the loss of a loved one. They work with clients to design tattoos that are meaningful and personal, and that will help to keep the memory of their loved one alive.

Memorial tattoos can take many different forms, from simple names and dates to complex and elaborate designs that incorporate symbols, images, and quotes that are meaningful to the client.

Fun Fact: Some memorial tattoo artists specialize in incorporating cremation ashes into their tattoos. This is a delicate process, and it is important to choose an artist who is experienced in this area.

Salary: $25,000-$40,000 per year.

ASH SCATTERING PILOT

Ash scattering pilots (sometimes called angel pilots) are licensed pilots who specialize in scattering the cremated remains of deceased people from airplanes. They work with families to choose a scattering location that is meaningful to the deceased, and then fly them to that location to scatter the ashes. They must be familiar with the laws and regulations regarding ash scattering in their area.

Fun Fact: Ash scattering is a popular practice in many cultures around the world. For example, in India, many people choose to have their ashes scattered in the Ganges River. In Japan, many people choose to have their ashes scattered in Mount Fuji.

Salary: $50,000-$70,000 per year.

ORGAN DONATION COORDINATOR

Organ donation coordinators work with patients and their families to coordinate the donation of organs and tissues after death. They educate patients and their families about the organ donation process, and help them make informed decisions about donation.

Fun Fact: Organ donation can save and improve the lives of up to eight people.

Salary: $40,000 to $600,000 per year.

COFFIN/CASKET/URN DESIGNER

Coffin, casket, and urn designers are responsible for creating the final resting place for the deceased. They work with families to create a coffin or casket that is both beautiful and meaningful, and that reflects the personality and life of the deceased.

Fun Fact: The world's most expensive coffin was made for King Tutankhamun of Egypt. It was made of solid gold and weighed over 250 pounds.

Salary: $35,000-$60,000 per year.

FORENSIC ANTHROPOLOGIST 🦴 🔧 💀 🔍

*Forensic anthropologist Douglas Owsley (left) and
APVA Preservation Virginia/ Historic Jamestowne
archaeologist (Danny Schmidt) discussing the double
burial of two European males. James Fort site, 1607.*
Smithsonian Institution, CC BY-SA 3.0, via Wikimedia
Commons

A forensic anthropologist is a professional who analyzes human
skeletal remains to determine information such as age, sex, and
cause of death. They may work for law enforcement agencies,
medical examiners offices, or universities.

Fun Fact: Forensic anthropology has been used to help solve some of the world's most high-profile cases, such as the identification of the remains of the Romanov family in Russia and the victims of the 9/11 attacks in New York City.

Salary: $40,000 to $100,000 per year.

FORENSIC PATHOLOGISTS

Forensic pathologists are medical doctors who specialize in the examination of bodies to determine the cause and manner of death. They work with law enforcement and medical examiners to investigate deaths, and their findings can be used to identify the deceased, determine the circumstances of their death, and bring criminals to justice.

They may also be trained in specialized areas, such as natural disasters or aviation pathology.

Fun Fact: The first recorded autopsy was performed in China in 1249.

Salary: $170,000 to $220,000 per year.

CRYONICS TECHNICIAN

A professional who is trained to preserve human bodies at extremely low temperatures in the hopes of reviving them in the future. Cryonics is a controversial field, and the scientific validity of cryopreservation is still a topic of debate among scientists.

Fun Fact: The first human cryopreservation was performed in 1967 on Dr. James Bedford, a psychology professor who died of cancer. Bedford's body is still cryopreserved to this day.

Salary: $30,000 to $60,000 per year.

FORENSIC ENTOMOLOGIST

A forensic entomologist analyzes the insects found on and around dead bodies. They study insects to determine the time of death, location of a crime scene, and other forensic information.

Fun Fact: The use of insects in forensic investigations dates back to ancient China, where it was recorded that flies were used to determine the cause of death.

Salary: $40,000 to $100,000 per year.

PET LOSS COUNSELOR

A trained professional who provides grief counseling and support to individuals who have lost a beloved pet.

Fun Fact: More than 60% of people with pets consider them to be family members.

Salary: $30,000-$60,000 per year

PET CREMATOR

Pet cremators prepare the bodies of deceased pets for cremation. They place the body in the cremation chamber and set the temperature and time. Once the cremation process is complete, they remove the cremated remains from the chamber and place them in an urn.

Fun Fact: Cremation is becoming increasingly popular for pets as well as people. In 2021, over 26% of pet owners chose cremation for their deceased pet.

Salary: $20,000-$35,000 per year.

PET TAXIDERMIST

Pet Taxidermists preserve the bodies of deceased pets through the art of taxidermy. This involves skinning, tanning, and mounting the animal in a lifelike pose, often with glass eyes to add to the realism.

Fun Fact: While dogs and cats are common, pet taxidermists can also work on a wide range of animals, from birds and rabbits to more exotic pets like reptiles.

Salary: $30,000 to $50,000 per year.

6

DIRTY JOBS: THE GROSS, THE GRITTY, AND THE GRUESOME

While some jobs may seem glamorous and comfortable, there are others that are downright dirty, gritty, or even gruesome.

In this chapter, we'll venture into the world of jobs that require getting down and dirty, handling things that others would find repulsive, or working in challenging and sometimes hazardous conditions. From sewer divers who brave the murky depths to plumbers who unclog the toughest blockages, these jobs are not for the faint of heart.

SEWAGE DIVER 🤿💩

Sewage divers plunge into the deep, dark depths of sewage systems to perform maintenance, unclog blockages, and repair leaks. Other names include wastewater divers and drain divers.

Fun Fact: The job of a sewage diver is considered one of the most dangerous professions in the world, with potential risks including drowning, exposure to toxic gases, and infection from harmful pathogens.

Salary: $60,000 to $100,000 per year.

FATBERG DIVER 💩🏊💩

Similar to a sewage diver, there's a specific job for someone to dive into sewer systems to remove blockages known as "fatbergs" which are made up of solid waste and fats that have accumulated in the sewer over time. These blockages can cause significant damage to the sewer system, and the job of a Fatberg Diver is to remove the blockage and prevent any further damage.

Fun Fact: The largest fatberg ever recorded was found in Whitechapel, London in 2017. It was made up of congealed fat, oil, and other waste that had been flushed down the drains. It weighed 130 tons and was 820 feet or 250 meters long. Just to put that into perspective 130 tons is the weight of 26 elephants or 100 cars and a city bus is 40 feet or 12 meters long and So this record-breaking fat burg measured 20 city buses long and weighed the same as 26 elephants or 100 cars.

This massive fatberg wreaked havic by causing a sewage blockage that then flooded streets and homes in the area. It took several weeks for workers to remove the record-breaking fatberg.

Salary: $60,000 to $100,000 per year.

BED BUG EXTERMINATOR

A professional who specializes in identifying and eliminating bed bug infestations in homes, hotels, and other buildings. These pests are notoriously difficult to get rid of, and often require a combination of chemical treatments and thorough cleaning to eliminate completely.

Fun Fact: Bed bugs have been around for thousands of years and were even mentioned in ancient Greek literature!

Salary: $35,000 to $60,000 per year.

CRIME SCENE CLEANER 🪧

Crime scene cleaners, also known as forensic cleaners, are responsible for cleaning up and decontaminating crime scenes, biohazardous materials, and other hazardous waste. They work closely with law enforcement officials and follow strict safety protocols to ensure that the area is safe and free from any harmful materials.

Fun Fact: On average, the cost of crime scene cleanup is between $1,000 and $10,000. The cost all depends on the size of the scene, the type of crime, and the how much decontamination is required.

Salary: $25,000 to $70,000 per year.

GASTROENTEROLOGIST (AKA POOP DOCTOR) 💩👨‍⚕️👩‍⚕️

Gastroenterologists are medical doctors who specialize in the digestive system and related organs. While they do deal with the unpleasant aspects of digestion, such as gas and bloating, they also help diagnose and treat more serious conditions like ulcers, inflammatory bowel disease, and even cancer. So, while they may be jokingly referred to as "poop doctors," they play an important role in keeping our digestive system healthy.

Fun Fact: Gastroenterologists also treat a range of other conditions, from acid reflux to pancreatitis.

Salary: $200,000 to $400,000 per year.

PROCOTOLOGIST (AKA BUTT DOCTOR)

Proctologists bravely go where few doctors dare to venture! A proctologist, also known as a colorectal surgeon, is a medical doctor who specializes in diagnosing and treating diseases of the rectum, anus, and colon. They perform procedures such as colonoscopies, biopsies, and surgeries to treat conditions like colon cancer, hemorrhoids, and inflammatory bowel disease.

Fun Fact: Proctologists often have a good sense of humor and may use puns or jokes related to their profession.

Salary: $200,000 to $400,000 per year.

MEDICAL WASTE DISPOSAL SPECIALIST

Medical waste disposal specialists are responsible for safely collecting, transporting, and disposing of medical waste generated from healthcare facilities. They ensure that medical waste is properly treated and disposed of in accordance with regulations to prevent contamination and harm to the environment and public health.

Medical waste can include anything from used needles to surgical gloves to bodily fluids, and improper disposal can pose serious health risks.

Fun Fact: The United States generates about 2.5 million tons of medical waste each year.

Salary: $40,000 to $60,000 per year.

HAZMAT DIVER 🤿💀

US Navy Hazmat Diver being cleaned and sanitized after completing a dive. Photo by Jmedanielle, CC BY-SA 3.0, via Wikimedia Commons

A professional diver who specializes in performing underwater tasks in hazardous environments such as contaminated water, chemical spills, and nuclear power plants. Their primary role is to ensure the safety of the environment, personnel, and public by detecting and mitigating hazardous materials underwater.

HAZMAT divers are required to wear special gear, including a sealed dry suit, full-face mask, and air supply system, to protect them from harmful contaminants in the water.

Fun Fact: It was in World War II when the first HAZMAT divers were used. HAZMAT diving is a specialized field with only a few thousand certified HAZMAT divers in the world.

Salary: $70,000 to $120,000 per year.

7

BEHIND THE SCREAMS: JOBS IN GHOSTLY ENTERTAINMENT

There's nothing quite like the thrill of being scared out of your wits, and haunted attractions and entertainment offer just that. But have you ever wondered who's behind the screams and scares?

In this chapter, we'll delve into the world of spirited careers that make haunted attractions and entertainment come to life. From makeup artists who create convincing special effects to scare actors who bring the frights to life, these jobs require skill, creativity, and a flair for the macabre.

So, brace yourself for a hair-raising journey as we explore the unusual and exciting jobs that make haunted attractions and entertainment so delightfully terrifying!

HAUNTED HOUSE DESIGNER

If you've ever visited a haunted house during Halloween season, you know how spooky and thrilling they can be. But have you ever wondered who comes up with all those terrifying scenes and jump scares? That's the job of a haunted house designer! They design, build, and create the creepy environments that scare the pants off of visitors.

Fun Fact: Haunted houses have been around for centuries, with roots in ancient pagan and Celtic traditions. Today, haunted house designers use cutting-edge technology, elaborate sets, and special effects to create spine-tingling experiences for visitors. Many designers draw inspiration from horror movies and popular culture to keep their designs fresh and innovative.

Salary: $30,000 to $60,000 per year.

HAUNTED ATTRACTION ACTOR

Haunted attraction actors play terrifying characters in haunted houses and other spooky events.

Fun fact: The haunted attraction industry is worth over $300 million in the US alone.

Salary: Minimum wage to $50 per hour. Since this is seasonal work, no average yearly salary has been included.

SCREAM PARK MANAGER

A scream park manager oversees the operation of a horror-themed amusement park, including hiring and managing staff, maintaining safety, and creating new attractions.

Fun Fact: The first scream park, the Erebus Haunted Attraction, opened in Michigan in 2000.

Salary: $40,000 to $100,000 per year.

ZOMBIE EXPERIENCE PERFORMER 🧟🧟‍♂️🧟‍♀️💀

Zombies. Photo by cottonbro studio via pexels.com

Zombie experience performers act as zombies in immersive experiences for fans of horror and the undead. Zombie Experience Performers may work in a variety of settings, from theme parks and haunted houses to film and television sets. They may also work as part of immersive theater productions or live events, where they interact with audiences and create a more interactive experience.

Fun Fact: Zombie experience performers often undergo extensive training to perfect their zombie performances. This can include not only physical training to create the right movements and body language, but also vocal training to master the distinctive growls and moans that are associated with zombies.

Salary: $30,000 to $60,000 per year.

ZOMBIE CHOREOGRAPHER

A zombie choreographer creates and teaches the movements and behaviors for actors playing zombies in movies, TV shows, and live events.

Fun Fact: Michael Jackson's "Thriller" music video popularized the idea of choreographed zombie movements.

Salary: $30,000 to $70,000 per year.

HORROR & GHOST TOUR GUIDE

A horror and or ghost tour guide leads groups through haunted locations, sharing stories and providing background on the history and folklore behind the sites. While many ghost tours operate year-round, there's often a significant surge in demand around October, leading up to Halloween. Guides might work back-to-back tours during this peak season.

Fun Fact: Some popular horror and ghost tours include the New Orleans Ghost Tour and the London Ghost Walk.

Salary: $20,000 to $50,000 per year.

HORROR MAKEUP ARTIST 🧟‍♀️🕯️💀🧛‍♀️👩‍🦰🕷️👁️👄

A horror makeup artist creates gruesome and terrifying looks for actors and performers in horror movies, haunted houses, and other horror-themed events.

Fun Fact: Famous horror makeup artists include Tom Savini and Rick Baker. Tom Savini is known for his work on *Friday the 13th*, *Dawn of the Dead*, and *The Fog*, Rick Baker is famous for his work on *Edward Scissorhands*, *The Thing*, and *An American Werewolf in London.*

Salary: $25,000 to $75,000 per year.

GHOST HUNTER 👻🔍📳📷💀🎥🧟‍♂️✔️

A ghost hunter or paranormal investigator, investigates paranormal activity in haunted locations, using a variety of tools such as electromagnetic field or EMF meters, infrared cameras, and electronic voice phenomena or EVP recorders.

While pop culture often portrays ghost hunting as a strictly nighttime activity, many investigations take place during the day, especially if the reported occurrences happen in daylight.

Fun Fact: The TV show *Ghost Hunters* popularized the idea of ghost hunting as a career.

Salary: $20,000 to $50,000 per year.

CREEPY DOLL MAKER

A creepy doll maker creates dolls and other toys with a creepy or unsettling aesthetic, often used in haunted houses or horror-themed events.

Fun Fact: Creepy dolls have been popularized in horror movies, such as *Annabelle* and *Chucky*.

Salary: $20,000 to $60,000 per year.

8

UNCOMMON OCCUPATIONS IN AVIATION

Airports are bustling centers of travel and commerce, but did you know that they're also home to some of the most unusual and unexpected jobs out there?

In this chapter, we'll take a behind-the-scenes look at the airport industry and discover the quirky and often-overlooked roles that keep planes flying and passengers moving.

BIRD CONTROL OFFICER

Bird control officers (BCOs) use various techniques to scare birds away from airport runways, preventing bird strikes and ensuring safe flights. BCOs may use a range of tools and equipment in their work, including bird traps, noisemakers, flares, netting, and even lasers. They must be knowledgeable about the regulations and best practices governing wildlife management in airport environments.

Fun Fact: The Chicago O'Hare International Airport hired the first bird control officer in 1964. There are now around 500 bird control officers at airports around the world.

Salary: $40,000 to $60,000 per year.

AERONAUTICAL INFORMATION SPECIALIST 🛩

Aeronautical information specialists (AIS) collect, analyze, and disseminate crucial flight data for pilots and air traffic controllers. They're like the air travel librarians, maintaining the ultimate resource for smooth and safe flying!

Fun Fact: The demand for AIS professionals is expected to grow in the coming years, due to the increasing complexity of the aviation industry and the need for accurate and reliable aeronautical information.

Salary: $60,000 to $90,000 per year.

AIRPORT WILDLIFE BIOLOGIST 🐦🦉🐍🦔🦆🦜🦫

Airport wildlife biologists monitor and manage wildlife populations around airports to minimize the risk of animal-related incidents. They may work for airports, government agencies, or private consulting firms. They must have a strong background in biology, ecology, and wildlife management, and be able to apply this knowledge to the unique challenges of airport environments.

Airport wildlife biologists may use a variety of techniques to manage wildlife populations, including habitat modification, noise deterrents, and even trained birds of prey.

Fun Fact: The Dallas/Fort Worth International Airport hired the first airport wildlife biologist in 1979. There are now over 100 airport wildlife biologists working at airports around the world.

Salary: $50,000 to $80,000 per year.

RUNWAY RUBBER REMOVAL SPECIALIST

Runway rubber removal specialists clean airport runways by removing rubber deposits left by aircraft tires during landing. They're like the runway's cleanup crew, keeping these pathways in tip-top shape for all those landings and takeoffs!

Rubber removal is typically done using specialized equipment, such as high-pressure water jets, mechanical scrubbers, or chemical solvents. The equipment used can vary depending on the type of runway and the extent of the rubber buildup.

Fun Fact: On average, airport runways need to be resurfaced every 10-15 years due to rubber deposit build-up. It can cost anywhere from $100,000 to $1 million per year to remove runway rubber.

Salary: $40,000 to $65,000 per year.

IN-FLIGHT MEDICAL ESCORT

In-flight medical escorts accompany and provide medical care to patients during air transportation. These escorts may be medical professionals like doctors or nurses, or they may be trained medical escorts who specialize in air travel.

Many airlines and travel companies offer in-flight medical escort services as part of their travel packages. These services can be especially helpful for elderly or passengers with disabilities, as well as those with chronic medical conditions.

Fun Fact: In-flight medical escorts are often called "sky nurses" and the most common medical emergencies they deal with are fainting, allergic reactions, and heart problems. They must also be trained to manage medical situations when experiencing turbulence.

Salary: $50,000 to $90,000 per year.

AIRCRAFT DECOMMISSIONER

Aircraft decommissioners, also known as aircraft dismantlers or recyclers, are professionals who are responsible for dismantling and recycling retired aircraft. They are also often referred to as "aircraft surgeons," due to the precision and skill required to dismantle an aircraft without damaging any of its parts or components.

Before an aircraft is decommissioned, it undergoes a process to ensure it's safe. This includes draining all fluids, neutralizing any ejection seat charges, and removing hazardous materials.

Fun Fact: In some cases, retired aircraft are not completely dismantled, but instead are repurposed for other uses like museums, restaurants, or even homes! Decommissioned aircraft or their parts are often used in movie sets and TV shows.

Salary: $45,000 to $70,000 per year.

AIRPORT ART CURATOR

Airport art curators plan, manage, and oversee art installations and exhibitions within airport terminals. They're like the airport's own gallery managers, turning terminals into fascinating artistic spaces!

Many airports around the world are known for their impressive art collections and installations. For example, Miami International Airport has a renowned art program that includes more than 80 installations and works by over 60 artists.

Fun Fact: San Francisco International Airport has an extensive art collection, including pieces by famous artists like Wayne Thiebaud and Sol LeWitt.

Salary: $45,000 to $75,000 per year.

RUNWAY INSPECTOR

Runway inspectors examine airport runways and taxiways for damage, debris, and safety hazards. Runway inspectors often use specialized equipment to inspect airport surfaces, such as high-speed cameras and laser measurement tools. These tools help inspectors identify any damage or wear on the runway surface that could potentially be hazardous to aircraft.

Fun Fact: Use of technology is becoming increasingly common in this profession. For example, some airports use drones for runway inspections, which can provide a bird's eye view and help detect issues that may not be visible at ground level.

Salary: $45,000 to $70,000 per year.

IN-FLIGHT CHEF

An inflight chef and flight attendant attend to Business Class passengers on Austrian Airlines flights. Photo by Austrian Airlines from Austria, CC BY-SA 2.0, via Wikimedia Commons

In-flight chefs are responsible for creating menus, sourcing ingredients, and preparing meals that meet the specific dietary requirements and preferences of passengers. They may work in a special galley kitchen on the plane, or they may prepare meals in advance and reheat them during the flight. Taste buds and the sense of smell behave differently at high altitudes. In-flight chefs have to design their recipes with stronger flavors and seasonings to compensate for this change.

Fun Fact: Some airlines offer in-flight cooking classes, where passengers can learn how to prepare dishes from their on-board chef. For example, Etihad Airways offers a "Flying Chef" program, where passengers can take a cooking class with one of the airline's chefs during their flight.

Salary: $45,000 to $80,000 per year.

PET TRAVEL AGENT 🐾✈️🐶🐱🐰🐢🐹💼

Pet travel agents arrange and manage the transportation of pets on flights, ensuring they are cared for, and comply with regulations. Pet travel agents may work with a variety of different animals, including dogs, cats, birds, and even exotic pets like reptiles and monkeys.

With more people traveling with their pets than ever before, pet travel agents are becoming an increasingly popular and in-demand profession.

Fun Fact: Many pet travel agents have backgrounds in veterinary medicine or animal behavior, and can provide expert advice on how to keep pets safe and comfortable while traveling.

Salary: $35,000 to $60,000 per year.

CUSTOMS CANINE HANDLER 🛂🐕🐾👮👮💼🔍

Customs canine handlers train and work with sniffer dogs, also known as detector dogs, to detect illegal substances and items in luggage and cargo. They're like the dynamic duos of airport security, teaming up with their furry partners to keep us all safe!

Fun Fact: Detector dogs come in a variety of breeds, including German Shepherds, Labrador Retrievers, and Beagles. These breeds are often chosen for their intelligence, trainability, and strong sense of smell.

Salary: $40,000 to $75,000 per year.

AIRPORT BEEKEEPER

Many airports have started keeping bees on their property as a way to support local ecosystems, promote sustainable practices, and even produce honey that can be sold or used in airport restaurants and cafes.

Airport beekeepers are often local bee enthusiasts or members of local bee associations, meaning the world of aviation intersects with local environmental efforts.

Fun Fact: Some airports have named their beehives after famous aviators or aviation-related terms. For example, Chicago O'Hare International Airport has a beehive named "Buzz Aldrin," while Vancouver International Airport has a hive named "The Beeport."

Salary: $35,000 to $60,000 per year.

BAGGAGE REPAIR TECHNICIAN

Baggage repair technicians fix damaged luggage and ensure that passengers' belongings are secure during travel. They're like the luggage doctors, stitching up suitcases and making them good as new!

Baggage repair technicians may also have the opportunity to travel to different airports and work with a variety of airlines, providing a unique and dynamic work environment.

Fun Fact: The most common type of damage that baggage repair technicians see is broken handles. This is because handles are often the weakest part of a suitcase.

Salary: $35,000 to $55,000 per year.

WING WALKER

Two wing walkers in Birmingham, UK in 2015. Photo by Tony Hisgett from Birmingham, UK, CC BY 2.0, via Wikimedia Commons

Wing walkers are thrill-seeking stunt performers who walk or perform acrobatic moves on the wings of flying airplanes. This job dates back to the 1920s and 1930s, when barnstorming pilots would perform daring stunts to entertain crowds at air shows. Today, wing walking is a popular attraction at air shows and aviation events around the world.

Many wing walkers have backgrounds in gymnastics, dance, or other physical disciplines.

Fun Fact: The most famous wing walker was Ormer Locklear. Locklear was a daredevil in 1920 who performed many dangerous stunts, including flying upside down and walking on the wingtip.

Salary: $40,000 to $65,000 per year.

AIRPORT HYDROLOGIST

Airport hydrologists study water-related issues around airports, such as stormwater management and drainage systems. Hydrologists may work for airports, government agencies, or private consulting firms. They may also work as independent contractors.

Hydrologists must have a strong background in hydrology, environmental science, and water resources management.

Fun Fact: There are over 1,000 airport hydrologists employed at airports around the world.

Salary: $50,000 to $85,000 per year.

IN-FLIGHT YOGA INSTRUCTOR

In-flight yoga instructors lead yoga and meditation sessions for passengers to help them relax and stay comfortable during long flights. In-flight yoga classes are typically offered as part of an airline's premium cabin services, and may be available for an additional fee. Passengers may also bring their own yoga mats or other equipment.

Fun Fact: The first in-flight yoga class was offered by Air India in 2009. There are now over 20 airlines that offer in-flight yoga classes.

Salary: $40,000 to $70,000 per year.

9

QUIRKY CAREERS IN CUISINE

The world of food is full of endless possibilities and flavors, and it takes a diverse and creative workforce to keep the culinary world turning.

In this chapter, we'll explore the unconventional and sometimes surprising jobs that make up the culinary industry. From ice sculptors who craft stunning displays to professional food stylists who make every dish look picture-perfect.

CHEESE SCULPTOR

A cheese sculptor creates sculptures and designs out of cheese. They may work for events, creating sculptures for displays and exhibits. Or they may create unique designs for cheese manufacturers.

Fun fact: The largest cheese sculpture ever created was made in 2018 in Lousiana and featured an alligator in a chef's hat frying a turkey. It was made from a single block of aged chedder cheese. It weighed 3,121 pounds (1,415.66 kg).

Salary: $25,000 to $50,000 per year.

ESCARGOT FARMER

An escargot farmer is a person who raises snails for use in the culinary industry. Escargot, or cooked land snails, are considered a delicacy in some cultures and are a popular ingredient in many French dishes. Snails are generally raised for about six months before they are harvested and sold for consumption.

Fun Fact: Escargot farmers often use special pens or corrals to keep the snails contained and prevent them from escaping.

Salary: $100,000 per year.

EDIBLE INSECT FARMER

An edible insect farmer raises and harvests insects for human consumption. Insects are a rich source of protein and are becoming more popular as a food source. Edible insect farming is a growing industry, with companies like Entomo Farms and Aspire Food Group producing insects like crickets and mealworms for human consumption.

Fun Fact: In addition to roasting and frying insects to eat them, companies also grind them into flour for use in baked goods and protein bars!

Salary: $30,000 to $60,000 per year.

FOOD STYLIST

Food stylist. Photo by Taryn Elliott via pexels.com

A food stylist is responsible for making food look aesthetically pleasing for photographs, commercials, and movies. Some food stylists specialize in certain types of food, such as desserts or beverages, while others have expertise in specific cuisines.

Fun Fact: Food stylists use a variety of techniques to make food look its best, even using fake ice cream or mashed potatoes to stand in for real food.

Salary: $25,000 to $75,000 per year.

FLAVORIST

A flavorist is a professional who creates flavors for food and beverage products. Flavorists have a very strong sense of smell. They must be able to detect even the subtlest differences in flavor.

They use a variety of ingredients to develop unique and appealing flavors.

The flavor industry is a multi-billion-dollar industry, with companies like Givaudan, Firmenich, and IFF (International Flavors & Fragrances) employing hundreds of flavorists around the world.

Fun Fact: The average flavorist has a vocabulary of over 10,000 different flavor descriptors.

Salary: $50,000 to $150,000 per year.

PIZZAOLOGIST

A pizzaologist, also known as "pizzaiolo" or "pizzaiola," is a person who studies the art and science of pizza. They learn about the history of pizza, different types of pizza, and how to make the perfect pizza.

Fun Fact: Pizzaiolos are often known for their showmanship and skill in tossing and stretching pizza dough. This technique, known as "acrobatic pizza tossing," has become a popular attraction at pizza competitions and events.

Salary: $25,000 to $50,000 per year.

GUMOLOGIST

A gumologist is a scientist who studies the properties and composition of chewing gum. They work for gum manufacturers, researching and developing new flavors and textures.

Fun fact: Chewing gum was originally made from tree sap. The flavor of bubblegum is actually a blend of banana, cherry, and strawberry.

Salary: $60,000 to $90,000 per year.

OYSTER SHUCKER

An oyster shucker is a professional who opens oysters and prepares them for consumption. They can work in restaurants or at events. In some parts of the world, oyster shucking is still done by hand using traditional tools like an oyster knife and glove. However, many modern oyster farms use machines to shuck their oysters for efficiency and consistency.

Fun Fact: Oyster shucking competitions are held all over the world, with competitors vying for the title of fastest and most skilled shucker. The world record for shucking oysters is currently held by Patrick McMurray, who shucked 38 oysters in one minute!

Salary: $19,000 to $34,000 per year.

CAVIAR FARMER

A caviar farmer is a professional who raises sturgeon fish and harvests their eggs to make caviar. They need specialized equipment and knowledge to ensure the best possible product. The process of harvesting caviar involves gently massaging the eggs out of the sturgeon, then cleaning and salting them.

Fun Fact: Caviar farming can be a highly lucrative business. Caviar is one of the most expensive foods in the world, with prices ranging from hundreds to thousands of dollars per pound!

Salary: $50,000 to $100,000 or more per year.

PROFESSIONAL PICKLE PACKER

A professional pickle packer is responsible for packing and preserving pickles. They work in factories or production facilities, ensuring that the pickles are properly sealed and labeled.

Fun fact: Pickles are the only food that can be classified as both a fruit and a vegetable.

Salary: $25,000 to $35,000 per year.

10

NOT JUST VINO: THE DIVERSE SIPS OF A SOMMELIER

While the word "sommelier" may immediately bring to mind the elegant world of wine, with experts swirling and savoring each sip, this realm of taste mastery extends far beyond the vineyards.

In this chapter, we'll not only explore the refined expertise of wine sommeliers, but also dive into the diverse array of sommeliers who specialize in a surprising range of delights—from cheese and tea, to chocolate...and even water!

Let your taste buds celebrate as we embark on a delicious journey into the captivating universe of sommeliers in all their splendid variety!

The World of Wine

Wine sommelier examining wine. Photo via depositphotos.com

WINE STEWARD 🍷🏆🥇🍇🍾💨🍷🥄

A wine steward is a first level sommelier who assists customers in choosing wine to accompany their meal. They usually work in restaurants or hotels and are responsible for maintaining the wine inventory.

Fun Fact: The term "sommelier" actually comes from the French word "soumelier," which means "pack animal driver." Sommeliers were originally responsible for transporting supplies, including wine, for the French royalty. Over time, the role of the sommelier evolved to include more wine-related duties, such as selecting, storing, and serving wine.

Salary: Around $37,000 per year.

ASSISTANT SOMMELIER

An assistant sommelier is a more experienced sommelier who is responsible for developing wine lists, training staff, and working with the head sommelier to ensure the wine service is impeccable.

Fun Fact: The world's oldest bottle of wine was discovered in Germany in 1867. The bottle is dated to between 325 and 350 AD, making it over 1,700 years old. The bottle is made of dark green glass and is sealed with a wax coating. It is thought to have contained a red wine, but the wine has long since evaporated. The bottle is now on display at the Historical Museum of the Palatinate in Speyer, Germany.

Salary: Around $50,000 per year.

CERTIFIED SOMMELIER

A certified sommelier is a professional sommelier who has passed an exam administered by the Court of Master Sommeliers. They are responsible for selecting and serving wine, as well as training staff and managing the wine cellar.

Fun Fact: The Court of Master Sommeliers was established in the United Kingdom in 1969 to provide a recognized standard of excellence in wine service.

Salary: Around $70,000 per year.

MASTER SOMMELIER

A master sommelier is the highest level of sommelier certification and is recognized as one of the most prestigious titles in the wine industry. They are responsible for managing wine programs in top-tier restaurants and hotels, as well as teaching and training other sommeliers.

Fun Fact: There are currently only 274 master sommeliers in the world, with the majority of them residing in the United States.

Salary: $150,000 to $400,000 per year.

WINE BUYER 🍷 💰 💼 📋 👨‍🔧 👩‍🔧 🍇 🥖

A wine buyer is responsible for selecting and purchasing wine for a restaurant, hotel, or wine retailer. They work closely with suppliers and distributors to ensure that the wine inventory meets the needs of their customers.

Fun Fact: The world's largest wine producer is Italy, followed by France and Spain.

Salary: Around $70,000 per year.

WINE EDUCATOR 🍸 🎓 📚 👨‍🏫 👩‍🏫 🍇 🥖 👨‍🎓

A wine educator is responsible for teaching and training others about wine, including sommeliers, wine buyers, and the general public. They may work for wine schools, wine companies, or as independent consultants.

Fun Fact: The oldest continuously operating winery in the world is the Weingut Staffelter Hof winery in Germany, which has been in operation since 862 AD.

Salary: Around $60,000 per year.

Other Sommeliers

WATER SOMMELIER

A water sommelier is a professional who specializes in water tasting, and can identify the different flavors and characteristics of various types of water. They also advise restaurants and hotels on water pairings.

Fun Fact: In 2017, the world's best water sommelier was named at the Fine Water Summit in Stockholm, Sweden.

Salary: Around $50,000 per year.

TEA SOMMELIER

A tea sommelier is an expert in teas, including their origin, brewing methods, and flavor profiles. They may work in tea shops or advise restaurants on tea pairings.

Fun fact: The world's first tea sommelier certification program was launched in 2003 in Canada.

Salary: Around $40,000 to $60,000 per year.

CHOCOLATE SOMMELIER

A chocolate sommelier is an expert in all things chocolate, including its origins, varieties, and pairings with other foods and beverages. They may work in specialty chocolate shops, advise restaurants on dessert menus, or lead chocolate tasting events.

A chocolate sommelier is different than a chocolatier. A chocolate sommelier focuses on the appreciation of chocolate, while a chocolatier focuses on the creation of chocolate.

Fun Fact: In 2019, the world's first chocolate sommelier competition was held in Paris, France.

Salary: Around $40,000 to $60,000 per year.

CHEESE SOMMELIER

A cheese sommelier is an expert in cheeses, including their origin, production, and pairing with wine and other foods. They may work in cheese shops, advise restaurants on cheese plates, or lead cheese-tasting events. The first virtual cheese sommelier competition was held in the United Kingdom in 2020.

Fun Fact: The most expensive and rarest cheese in the world is made from a combination of the milk of Balkan donkeys and goat's milk and is called Pule. It's produced by only one farm in the world in Serbia. Pule costs around $600 or more per pound.

Salary: Around $40,000 to $60,000 per year.

WHISKEY SOMMELIER

Much like other sommeliers, they have an in-depth knowledge of whiskey production, regions, aging processes, and flavor profiles. They may work at high-end restaurants, distilleries, specialty liquor stores, dedicated whiskey bars, luxury hotels, and cruise ships.

Fun Fact: There are "whiskey libraries" in parts of the world where patrons can "check out" samples from thousands of bottles, some of which might be extremely rare.

Salary: Around $40,000 to $70,000 per year, but could be much higher depending on their experience, reputation, and location.

HONEY SOMMELIER

A honey sommelier is an expert in different types of honey, including their flavor, aroma, and nutritional properties. Honey sommeliers can identify over 300 different types of honey. Each type of honey has its own unique flavor profile, which is influenced by the type of flowers that the bees have visited.

Honey sommeliers can pair honey with food and drinks in the same way that wine sommeliers pair wine with food. They may work in specialty food stores or advise restaurants on honey pairings.

Fun Fact: The world's first honey sommelier certification program was launched in 2012 in Italy.

Salary: Around $50,000 to $70,000 per year.

MEAT SOMMELIER

Meat sommeliers are trained to taste and evaluate meat in a similar way to wine sommeliers. They consider the meat's appearance, aroma, taste, texture, and doneness. They also take into account the meat's breed, cut, and aging process.

Meat sommeliers can identify over 100 different cuts of meat from different animals. They may work in specialty butcher shops or advise restaurants on meat selection and preparation.

Fun fact: The world's first meat sommelier certification program was launched in 2017 in Japan.

Salary: Around $50,000 to $70,000 per year.

BEER SOMMELIER

Beer sommelier in Nebraska, USA. Photo by Shelby L. Bell, CC BY 2.0, via Wikimedia Commons

A beer sommelier, also known as a beer maven and cicerone, is an expert in different types of beer, including their ingredients, brewing methods, and flavor profiles. Beer sommeliers can identify over 1,000 different types of beer. They may work in breweries, advise restaurants on beer pairings, or lead beer-tasting events. Beer sommeliers are often involved in the development of new beers.

Fun Fact: The world's first beer sommelier certification program was launched in 2004 in Belgium.

Salary: Around $40,000 to $60,000 per year.

OLIVE OIL SOMMELIER

An olive oil sommelier is an expert in different types of olive oil, including their flavor, aroma, and quality. Olive oil sommeliers can identify over 500 different types of olive oil. They may work in specialty food stores or advise restaurants on olive oil pairings.

Fun Fact: The world's first olive oil sommelier certification program was launched in 2011 in Italy.

Salary: Around $50,000 to $70,000 per year.

SAKE SOMMELIER

A Sake sommelier is an expert in Japanese sake, a fermented rice beverage. Sake is one of the oldest alcoholic beverages in the world, with a history dating back over 2,000 years. Sake sommeliers can identify over 1,000 different types of sake. They may work in restaurants, bars, retail stores, sake breweries, and educational institutions.

Beyond just pouring sake, there are various traditional rituals and etiquettes associated with serving sake, such as the "tokkuri" (sake flask) tilt method. A sake sommelier is well-versed in these traditions.

Fun Fact: There are various levels of certification in Japan, similar to wine sommeliers. The highest level is known as a "Master of Sake," which is a difficult and prestigious title to achieve. There have only been just over 500 people in the world who have achieved this title.

Salary: $35,000 to $90,000 per year.

11

FORGOTTEN AND FASCINATING
JOBS OF THE PAST

Now let's journey back in time to explore the weird and wonderful occupations that people once had. From lamplighters who illuminated city streets to knocker-uppers who served as human alarm clocks, these jobs may seem strange to us today but played important roles in the daily lives of people long ago.

Most of the salaries in this section are based on estimates using a six-day workweek, which was common until about the 1930's and then trying to relate that to what that would be today accounting for inflation. They are only rough estimates.

For context, in the U.S. in 1900 to 1909, wage-earning men made an average of $11.16 per week and wage-earning women made an average of $6.17 per week in 1905.

KNOCKER-UPPERS ⏰🕰️🐀🥢🛏️🧱

Knocker-uppers woke people in the morning by tapping on their bedroom windows with a long stick, or shooting peas at the glass. The role of Knocker-uppers dates back to the 19th and early 20th centuries. They would typically work in urban areas and serve a variety of clients, including factory workers, office workers, and students. They were the human alarm clocks before the digital age!

Fun Fact: In the United Kingdom, the Knocker-uppers is still remembered as an important part of local history and culture.

Salary: Around $2-$5 per week or $104-$260 annually in the early 1900s. Comparable to $3,200 to $8,000 per year today.

LOG DRIVER 🪵🪚🏞️🌊🌲🌳👷👨‍🌾

Log drivers on the Klarälven river flowing through Norway and Sweden. Photo by User Obli on en.wikipedia, Public domain, via Wikimedia Commons

Log drivers guided large bundles of logs downriver to sawmills by standing on the floating logs and using poles to steer. They would need to navigate rapids, dams, and other obstacles, as well as ensure that the logs did not get stuck or jammed along the way.

Fun Fact: In some parts of the world, such as Canada and the United States, Log Driving still exists as a small industry or a recreational activity, although it is not as common as it once was.

Salary: Comparable to $40,000 to $60,000 per year today.

LECTOR

Lectors read aloud from books or newspapers to factory workers to keep them entertained and informed during their shifts. This practice was particularly common in the late 19th and early 20th century, before the widespread availability of radio and other forms of entertainment. Lectors were especially associated with the cigar-making industry.

Fun Fact: The tradition of lectors in cigar factories can be traced back to the mid-19th century in Cuba. It later spread to other cigar-producing regions like Florida, especially in the Ybor City area of Tampa.

Salary: Lectors typically earned a wage that was competitive with other factory workers. In some cases, they were paid by the workers themselves, who contributed to a fund to cover the lector's salary. Comparable to $25,000 to $35,000 per year today.

ICE CUTTER

Ice cutters harvested large blocks of ice from frozen lakes and rivers to be used for refrigeration before the advent of electric refrigerators. Before the invention of refrigerators, ice cutters were in high demand, especially during the summer months. Ice was transported a variety of ways including horse-drawn wagons and railroad cars. Horse-drawn wagons were used to transport ice from the icehouse to businesses and homes. The wagons were insulated with sawdust or straw to help keep the ice from melting.

Railroad cars were used to transport ice long distances. The cars were insulated with sawdust or straw to help keep the ice from melting.

Fun Fact: Fredric Tudor, also known as The Ice King, was the first international ice trader. He began exporting ice from Boston, Massachusetts in 1806 to places like India and Martinique. He would ship 146,000 tonnes of ice around the world each year.

Salary: Around $0.10-$0.15 per hour in the early 1900s. Comparable to $40,000 to $60,000 per year today.

LEECH COLLECTOR

Leech collectors gathered medicinal leeches from swampy areas for use in bloodletting, a common medical treatment in the past. The role of Leech collector dates back to ancient times, when leeches were believed to have healing properties and were used to treat a variety of ailments, from headaches to skin diseases. Leech collectors would typically search for leeches in freshwater ponds and streams, using their bare hands or special tools to collect the slimy creatures.

Fun Fact: While the practice of bloodletting with leeches has largely disappeared in modern medicine, leeches are still used in some surgical procedures as a means of reducing blood clots and promoting healing.

Salary: Comparable to $35,000 to $50,000 per year today.

LAMPLIGHTER

Lamplighter in Sweden. Photo by Gunnar Lanz, Public domain, via Wikimedia Commons.

Lamplighters lit, extinguished and maintained gas street lamps before electric streetlights were introduced. It took hours every day to light and extinguish every street lamp. Lamp Lighters were also known as "leeries." The role of Lamplighter dates back to the 18th century, when street lighting was first introduced in urban areas. Lamplighters would typically carry a long pole with a hook on the end, which they would use to light the gas lamps by hand.

Fun Fact: In the early days of gas lighting, the job was seen as dangerous due to the risk of explosions. Lamplighters also often had to work in hazardous conditions, such as during heavy rain or snowstorms.

Salary: Around $1-$2 per day or $312-$624 annually in the 1800s. Comparable to $9,600 to $19,300 per year today.

PINSETTER

Pinboys working in Brooklyn, New York. Photo by Lewis Wickes Hine, 1874-1940, photographer., Public domain, via Wikimedia Commons.

Pinsetters manually reset bowling pins and returned balls to players before the invention of automated pinsetters.

Fun Fact: Pinsetters were often young boys, and the job was known for its low pay and long hours.

Salary: Around $2-$3 per week or $104-$156 annually in the 1930s. Comparable to $2,300 to $3,500 per year today.

RAT CATCHER 🐀🔪🐕🐀🐀🐍🪣🐀🤠

Professional rat catchers in Sydney, Australia in 1900. Photo by Photographic Collection from Australia, CC BY 2.0, via Wikimedia Commons

Rat catchers trapped and exterminated rats in urban areas to control the rodent population and prevent disease. Rat catchers often used ferrets or dogs to help them catch the rats. In 19th century England, rat-catchers were often celebrated figures, and some were even hired to clear out rat infestations in famous landmarks such as the Houses of Parliament.

Today, this job has evolved into pest control professionals and using more sophisticated methods and technologies to control rat populations. This includes humane traps, surveillance equipment, and pest management practices that focus on prevention and control without excessive reliance on chemicals. Their role is not just about extermination but also about education, to help people understand best practices to prevent infestations.

Fun Fact: In Victorian England, Rat Catchers would often display their captured rats in public as proof of their success.

Salary: Around $1-$2 per day or $312-$624 annually in the 1900s. Comparable to $9,600 to $19,300 per year today.

TOWN CRIER 🔔🗣📣

Town criers announced important news and events in public spaces before newspapers and broadcasting were widespread. They were the original news anchors, bringing the latest scoop straight to the streets! Town criers were common in medieval Europe, and the tradition still continues in some places today, albeit in a more ceremonial role.

Fun Fact: Town criers often wore flamboyant clothing to draw attention to themselves.

Salary: Around $1-$2 per day or $312-$624 annually in the 1900s. Comparable to $9,600 to $19,300 per year today.

RESURRECTIONIST 🪦 💀 🔪 🪦

*Iron Mortsafe used to protect newly buried bodies from being dug up
and sold to medical schools. Photo by Eileen Henderson / Colinton
Mortsafe CC-BY-SA-2.0, via Wikimedia Commons*

Resurrectionists (or body snatchers) would illegally dig up dead
bodies to obtain recently buried corpses and sell them to
medical schools for dissection and research. This was particularly prevalent in the 18th and 19th centuries.

When the demand for cadavers (dead bodies) for medical
research and education exceeded the supply, sometimes people
would even murder other people to get the body.

Fun Fact: William Burke, one of the more infamous resurrec-
tionist, was found guilty of of over 16 murders, hanged for his
crimes, and his body was publicly dissected. His skeleton was
given to the Anatomical Museum of the Edinburgh Medical
School where it remains still as of 2023.

Payment: Records show that in 1828 in London, body snatchers were paid per corpse and the price per corpse could vary. They were paid anywhere from two to twenty guineas or more per corpse. One guinea works out to be £1.05 today or $1.37. Compared to the one guinea a manservant to a wealthy household made in a week during that same time period, selling corpses could be very profitable.

LINKBOY

Linkboys carried torches or lanterns (called links) to light the way for pedestrians in urban areas before street lighting was common. Linkboys were common in 18th and 19th century London. While many linkboys offered a genuine service, others had a reputation for leading unsuspecting individuals into dark alleys to be robbed.

Linkboys were typically young boys, often from poorer backgrounds. It was a way for them to make a little money, but it wasn't a particularly high-paying or prestigious profession.

Fun Fact: Linkboys have been mentioned in literature to set the scene of nighttime in older cities. For instance, they appear in works of Charles Dickens and William Thackeray.

Payment: Linkboys usually earned their income through tips from the people they assisted.

SWITCHBOARD OPERATOR

Switchboard operators connected phone calls by manually plugging wires into a switchboard before automated systems were developed. Switchboard operators were mostly women, and the job was often seen as a stepping stone to higher positions in the telephone company.

Fun Fact: The first switchboard was invented in 1876 by Alexander Graham Bell's cousin, and the first operators were teenage boys.

Salary: Around $15-$20 per week or $780-$1,040 annually in the 1940s. Comparable to $13,300 to $17,700 per year today.

DAGUERREOTYPIST

Daguerreotypists can be considered the world's first commercial photographers, offering portraiture services to the public. Before this, capturing someone's likeness was a privilege mostly reserved for the wealthy, who could afford painted portraits.

Daguerreotypists created photographic images using an early photographic process of exposing silver-plated copper to light for different lengths of time, then carefully putting the image under the protection of glass. Daguerreotypes are unique, as each plate produced only one image, and there were no negatives or duplicates.

Early daguerreotypes required the subject to sit still for up to 15 minutes! This is why many subjects in daguerreotypes have a very stiff or stern expression. Devices called "posing stands" were used to keep subjects still during the exposure.

Fun Fact: The first authenticated image of Abraham Lincoln was a daguerreotype.

Salary: Comparable to $40,000 to $60,000 per year today.

CHIMNEY SWEEP 🧹🏠🔥💀💀🧹

*Chimney sweep in Germany between 1862 and 1868.
Photo by Rejlander, Oskar Gustav, Public domain, via
Wikimedia Commons*

Chimney sweeps were a common sight in cities during the 18th and 19th centuries. Chimney sweeps cleaned soot and debris from chimneys to prevent fires and maintain air quality in homes. Chimney sweeps often worked long hours in dangerous conditions, and were typically young boys or small men who could fit inside the narrow chimney flues.

While not as common, there are still people who work as chimney sweeps in some parts of the world today. In addition to cleaning chimneys, modern chimney sweeps also inspect chimneys and flues to ensure they are safe and in good working condition. They may also install or repair chimneys, fireplaces, or stoves, and provide advice on fire safety and proper use of heating equipment.

Fun Fact: In many countries, chimney sweeps were considered to be good luck symbols. It was believed that touching the buttons on a sweep's jacket, or carrying a chimney sweep charm, would bring good fortune.

Salary: Comparable to $25,000 to $40,000 per year today.

VOCODER OPERATOR

The vocoder is an electronic instrument that was developed in the early 20th century for use in telecommunications. It was later adopted by musicians as a tool for creating unique and distinctive vocal effects. The vocoder works by analyzing the frequency and amplitude of an audio signal, and using that information to manipulate another audio signal in real-time.

Vocoder operators encrypted and decrypted voice communications during World War II using a speech scrambler device.

Fun Fact: The vocoder is still used today in a wide variety of musical genres, and is often used to create robotic and other-worldly vocal effects.

Salary: Comparable to $45,000 to $70,000 per year today.

POWDER MONKEY

Powder monkey in the U.S. Navy. Photo by National Museum of the U.S. Navy, Public domain, via Wikimedia Commons

Powder monkey is a term that dates back to the 17th century and refers to the young boys who were responsible for carrying gunpowder to the cannons during battles at sea. These boys were usually between the ages of 10 and 18, and were often orphans or children from poor families who couldn't afford to raise them. The job was dangerous, and many Powder Monkeys were killed or injured in battle.

After the American-British War of 1812, boys under the age of twelve were no longer allowed to serve on U.S. Navy ships.

Fun Fact: Despite the risks, the job offered a chance for young boys to gain valuable experience at sea. While young boys were common, older men, especially those unfit for more physically demanding tasks on the ship, could also be employed as powder monkeys.

Salary: These boys were not given a salary, merely a bed, some clothes, and a basic education.

SLATE PENCIL MAKER

A person who manufactured pencils made of slate, a type of sedimentary rock that was commonly used for writing and drawing in the 19th and early 20th centuries. The role of slate pencil maker was important in its time, as pencils made of slate were durable, long-lasting, and could be erased and reused many times.

Slate pencil makers would typically work in small factories or workshops, using specialized tools and techniques to shape and sharpen the pencils from blocks of slate. They would then package the pencils for distribution and sale to schools, offices, and individuals.

Fun Fact: Slate pencil makers often had to work in dusty and dirty conditions, as the process of shaping and sharpening slate pencils produced a lot of dust and debris.

Salary: According to some sources, slate pencil makers in the United States in the early 20th century could earn as little as

$6.25 per week. Today, that works out to be about $200 a week or $10,400 per year.

HUMAN COMPUTER

A person who performed complex mathematical calculations by hand without the aid of electronic or mechanical devices. The role of human computer dates back to the early days of science and engineering, when the ability to perform accurate and precise calculations was essential for scientific discovery and technological advancement.

Human computers would typically work in teams, using pen and paper or other simple tools to perform calculations for various projects, such as calculating trajectories for rockets or analyzing astronomical data.

Fun Fact: Many of the early pioneers in computing were women who worked as human computers. This was particularly true in the United States during World War II, when women were recruited to work as human computers for the military.

Salary: In the early days of computing, human computers were often paid low wages and were considered to be low-level clerical workers. According to the book *Hidden Figures*, which tells the story of the African-American women who worked as human computers at NASA during the 1960s, the starting salary for these women was around $1,800 per year, which was well below the average salary for women in the United States at the time.

ELEVATOR OPERATOR

Elevator girl in 1917 in the US. Photo by Bain, Public domain, via Wikimedia Commons.

Elevator operators were responsible for manually operating elevators before automatic controls were invented. They would operate the controls and assist passengers with entering and exiting the elevator. Elevator operator positions were often filled by women, and this occupation provided an opportunity for women to enter the workforce in the late 19th and early 20th centuries.

Fun Fact: Elevator operators were known for their uniforms, which typically included a cap and a uniform with a badge indicating their position. They were also expected to maintain a high level of courtesy and professionalism in their interactions with passengers.

Salary: $12-$18 per week or $25,000 to $37,500 per year in today's money.

KEYPUNCH OPERATORS

Keypunch operators were essential workers from the 1960s to the 1980s. They entered data into IBM keypunch machines, which punched holes into punch cards known as a Hollerith cards. Computer operators then fed these cards into computers to generate bills, records, and other documents.

Keypunch Operators also worked in credit reporting offices where they sat at rows of desks with conveyor belts in between. Banks and Auto Dealers would call in to request credit reports on potential customers. An operator answered the phone, entered the client's questions into the system, and sent a punched card down the conveyor belt to the computer room. Inside, a Computer Operator processed the card, generating a credit report that was sent back to the original operator. The

Keypunch Operator would then read back the credit report to the caller.

These professionals were known for their precision and speed in data entry, and they worked in a variety of industries, including utilities, banking, and defense contracting.

Fun Fact: Skilled Keypunch Operators could type at impressive speeds, often reaching 10,000 to 12,000 keystrokes per hour.

Salary: Around $125 per week or $6,500 per year in 1965. Comparable to $63,375 per year today.

GONG FARMER (AKA NIGHT SOIL COLLECTOR)

A gong farmer, or night soil collector, was a person who collected human waste from households. The role of night soil collector dates back to ancient times, when human waste was used as fertilizer for crops. Night soil collectors would typically work at night, using buckets or carts to collect the waste from the homes of their clients. They would then transport the waste to a designated location, such as a farm or designated disposal site.

Night soil collectors often earned more than general laborers because of the hazardous and unpleasant nature of their work.

The term "gong farmer" comes from the Old English word "gang," meaning "to go" or "journey," and "gong" was a euphemism for a privy or outhouse. The "farmer" part of the title referred to their work collecting the waste, which could then be used as fertilizer for agricultural purposes.

With the development of modern plumbing and sewage systems in the late 19th and early 20th centuries, the role of Night soil collector largely disappeared in many parts of the world.

Fun Fact: They were sometimes referred to as "honey wagons" in the United States, due to the fact that the waste they collected was often used to fertilize crops, including plants used to produce honey.

Salary: According to some sources, night soil collectors in the United States in the early 20th century could earn as little as $0.10 per bucket of waste collected, with an estimated $1.50 to $4 per day.

Assuming a six-day workweek, which was common during that era, and 52 weeks a year (although they likely did not work every single day due to weather and other factors), we get an estimated annual range of $468 to $1,248. In today's U.S. dollars, accounting for inflation, that would be $14,508 to $38,688 per year.

12

UNIQUE OCCUPATIONS IN ROYAL COURTS

Throughout history, royal courts have been home to a fascinating array of peculiar professions that may seem strange or downright bizarre to us today. From silkworm farmers who ensured a steady supply of luxurious silk, to the groom of the stool responsible for the monarch's most private affairs, these often-overlooked roles played a significant part in the daily lives of kings, queens, and their courts.

In the old royal courts, many jobs were about honor and duty, not just pay. Because of this, and the lack of detailed old records, this chapter does not include salary information. But remember, being close to the throne had its own special perks!

For your royal context, it's important to note that many of the jobs and roles mentioned below pertain to the British monarchy. The official titles and role names may vary depending on the reigning monarch.

KEEPER OF THE KING'S STAMPS

The "Keeper of the King's Stamps" is a role that still exists today, and refers to the person who is responsible for managing the Royal Philatelic Collection, which is the official stamp collection of the British Royal Family. The Royal Philatelic Collection is one of the most extensive and valuable stamp collections in the world, with more than two million items dating back to the mid-19th century.

The Keeper of the King's Stamps is responsible for managing and preserving the collection, as well as acquiring new items and providing expert advice and guidance on philatelic matters. They work closely with other members of the royal household, as well as with stamp collectors and experts from around the world, to ensure that the collection is properly catalogued, conserved, and displayed.

Fun Fact: The role of Keeper of the King's Stamps has been held by members of the royal family themselves, including Queen Victoria, King George V, and King George VI. Today, the role is held by a professional philatelist appointed by King Charles III.

CHIEF ASTROLOGER

The Chief Astrologer was responsible for advising the king and queen on matters of astrology, and interpreting the stars for omens and predictions.

Fun Fact: Astrology was considered a legitimate science during the Renaissance period.

MASTER OF THE KING'S MUSIC 🎼🎶🎵🎹🎹

The Master of the King's Music was responsible for composing and performing music for the royal court and overseeing the king's musicians. Similar to other roles, when a queen holds the position of reigning monarch, this title is known as 'Master of the Queen's Music.'

Fun Fact: The position of Master of the King's Music dates back to the Tudor era in England. During the reign of King Henry VIII of England, the position of Master of the King's Music was held by William Cornysh, who was a talented composer and musician. Cornysh was reportedly so talented that he was able to compose new music on the spot when King Henry requested it.

KEEPER OF THE WARDROBE 👗👚🧥👕👕

The Keeper of the Wardrobe was responsible for managing the reigning monarch's clothing and ensuring their wardrobe was well-maintained and up-to-date. The position of Keeper of the Wardrobe dates back to the Middle Ages.

Fun Fact: During the reign of Queen Elizabeth I of England, the Keeper of the Wardrobe was held by Sir Walter Raleigh, who was also a famous explorer and poet. Raleigh was known for his impeccable fashion sense, and was often seen wearing elaborate clothing adorned with jewels and feathers.

COURT FOOL/JESTER 🎭🃏😀👥😄

The Court Fool, or Court Jester, was responsible for entertaining the king and queen and their guests with jokes, pranks, and satire. The Court Fool would perform a variety of humorous skits, songs, and dances, often at the expense of the other guests—or even the king or queen themselves. They would use a variety of props and costumes, and would often incorporate juggling, acrobatics, and other physical feats into their performances.

Fun Fact: Court Fools were often allowed to speak truth to power and offer criticisms of the monarchy without fear of retribution.

ROYAL FOOD TASTER

The Royal Food Taster was responsible for testing the king's or queen's food for poison and ensuring it was safe to eat.

Fun Fact: Poisoning was a common method of assassination in the past, making the role of Royal Food Taster a vital one.

KEEPER OF THE PRIVY SEAL

The Keeper of the Privy Seal was a high-ranking official in the royal household and was responsible for managing the reigning monarch's official seal and affixing it to important documents.

Fun Fact: The position of Keeper of the Privy Seal dates back to medieval times.

ROYAL CHIEF EMBROIDERER

The Royal Chief Embroiderer was responsible for overseeing the creation of elaborate embroidered designs for the royal household's clothing and furnishings. The position of Royal Chief Embroiderer still exists today and is a highly coveted one, and it is only awarded to the most skilled and experienced embroiderers.

Fun Fact: Caroline Rush is the current royal chief embroiderer for King Charles III. Rush is a textile artist and designer who has worked for the Royal Household for over 20 years. She has designed a number of pieces for the royal family, including the late Queen's Diamond Jubilee dress. Rush is responsible for designing and creating all of the King's official ceremonial clothing, including his coronation gown and state robes. She will also be responsible for overseeing the work of the Royal School of Needlework, which trains young people in the art of embroidery.

KEEPER OF THE KING'S APES

The Keeper of the King's Apes was responsible for managing and caring for the monarch's collection of exotic apes, which were often kept as pets and curiosities in royal households during the medieval and Renaissance periods. Similar to other roles, when a queen holds the position of reigning monarch, this title is known as 'Keeper of the Queen's Apes.'

Fun Fact: Apes were often dressed in human clothing and taught to perform tricks for the amusement of the court.

ROYAL PERFUMER

The Royal Perfumer was responsible for creating bespoke perfumes and scented products for the reigning monarch and their household. The role of Royal Perfumer was particularly important during the Renaissance and Baroque periods, when perfumes and other scented products were considered to be a symbol of wealth, power, and luxury.

Fun Fact: The art of perfumery dates back to ancient Egypt and was highly prized by royalty and the upper classes.

GRAND CARVER 🦌 🍖 👑 🍽️

The Grand Carver was responsible for carving and serving the reigning monarch's meat dishes at banquets and feasts. The Grand Carver would oversee the preparation and presentation of meat dishes, including roasts, steaks, and other cuts of meat. They would be responsible for ensuring that the meat was cooked to the appropriate level of doneness and was presented in an appealing and appetizing manner.

Fun Fact: The position of Grand Carver was particularly important in medieval and Renaissance times, when meat was a rare and expensive delicacy.

KEEPER OF THE KING'S WORMS 👤 🐛 👑

The Keeper of the King's Worms was responsible for cultivating silkworms and overseeing the production of silk for the king and queen's clothing. Silk production was a highly specialized and labor-intensive industry, and the Keeper of the King's Worms would have been a highly skilled and respected member of the royal household. They would have worked closely with other members of the royal household, including weavers, tailors, and seamstresses, to produce high-quality silk textiles for use in clothing and other luxury goods.

Like other positions, when a queen is the reigning monarch, this title becomes 'Keeper of the Queen's Worms.'

Fun Fact: Silk was a highly prized and expensive fabric during the Middle Ages and Renaissance.

MASTER OF THE KING'S BEARS & DOGS

The Master of the King's Bears and Dogs was a high-ranking courtier in the royal household and was responsible for caring for and training the king and queen's hunting dogs and overseeing the use of bears in bear-baiting events. Bear-baiting was a blood sport in which a chained bear was attacked by dogs. It was a popular form of entertainment in Britain from the 12th to the 19th centuries. As mentioned before, when a queen is the reigning monarch, this title becomes 'Master of the Queen's Bears & Dogs.'

Fun Fact: In addition to their work with hunting animals, the Master of the King's Bears and Dogs would also be responsible for managing other aspects of the royal household's animal collection, including birds of prey, exotic animals, and domestic livestock.

ROYAL FALCONRY MEWS KEEPER

The Royal Falconry Mews Keeper was responsible for caring for the king and queen's falcons and other birds of prey used for hunting. The term "mews" refers to the place where the birds were housed, and the term "falconry" refers to the practice of hunting with trained birds of prey.

Fun Fact: In medieval times, falconry was considered a sport of the nobility, and was used as a way to train birds of prey for hunting. The role of the Royal Falconer was considered an important one, as a well-trained bird of prey could mean the difference between success and failure on the hunt.

COURT PAINTER 🧑‍🎨🎨🎨

The Court Painter was responsible for creating portraits and other artwork for the reigning monarch and their household.

Fun Fact: Many famous artists, including Leonardo da Vinci and Michelangelo, worked as Court Painters during the Renaissance period.

GROOM OF THE STOOL 💩🚽👑

The Groom of the Stool was responsible for attending to the king's or queen's toileting needs and maintaining his/her private bathroom. When the role of the Groom of the Stool was associated with the queen, it was typically referred to as the "Lady of the Bedchamber" or a similar title.

People in this role were often required to wear specific attire while on duty, which was designed to be practical for their tasks while maintaining the dignity of the royal court.

Fun Fact: While the role of Groom of the Stool or Lady of the Bedchamber may seem unappealing to modern sensibilities, it was considered a highly prestigious position in medieval times. The Groom of the Stool was often a trusted confidante of the monarch, and was responsible for attending to the king's or queen's personal hygiene needs.

The royal "close stool" (1689-1702). Photo by Lobsterthermidor, Public domain, via Wikimedia Commons

13

OUTLANDISH OCCUPATIONS:
CUDDLERS & QUEUE-KEEPERS

Just when you thought you'd heard it all, we're about to introduce you to a world of even more unbelievable careers that will have you doing a double-take.

From professional queuers who wait in line so you don't have to, to cuddlers who offer a warm embrace for a living. And from fake patients who help doctors sharpen their skills, to human statues who bring art to life—these jobs are as quirky as they come. And that's not all—we'll also dive into the enchanting lives of professional mermaids and the spine-chilling performances of zombie experience actors.

So, brace yourself for an eye-opening journey as we uncover the fun and funky jobs that have been hiding in plain sight, proving that the working world is much more fascinating than you ever imagined!

PROFESSIONAL BRIDESMAID 🌿 💀 🕯 ⌇

Pofessional bridesmaid. Photo by Emma Bauso via pexels.com

A person who is hired to provide support and assistance to the bride and her bridal party during the wedding planning process and on the wedding day itself. Professional bridesmaids may perform a variety of tasks, such as helping to plan and organize the wedding, assisting with dress fittings and makeup, and providing emotional support and advice to the bride and her attendants.

Fun Fact: The concept of a professional bridesmaid is not new. In fact, in ancient Rome, bridesmaids were hired to dress like the bride and confuse evil spirits that were thought to be lurking around the ceremony.

Salary: Around $300 to $2,000 per wedding.

PROFESSIONAL BED TESTER

Bed testers sleep in various beds to test their comfort and quality for hotels or manufacturers.

Fun Fact: Some bed testers are required to sleep on the mattress for several days or even weeks to test the long-term durability and comfort of the product.

Salary: $30,000 to $60,000 per year.

PROFESSIONAL SLEEPER

Professional sleepers are paid to sleep for scientific studies, product testing, or hotel quality assurance. They also test out mattresses and beds for hotels and manufacturers to ensure they are comfortable and of high quality.

Fun Fact: NASA pays volunteers to sleep for 70 days straight to test the effects of space travel on the body.

Salary: $25,000 to $75,000 per year.

PROFESSIONAL MOURNER

Professional mourners, also known as moirologists, attend funerals and wakes to grieve alongside the family and provide emotional support. While the primary role might seem to be crying, professional mourners often have to sing lamentations, wail, or even roll on the ground, depending on the cultural and regional customs.

Fun Fact: The practice of hiring mourners can be traced back to ancient Egyptian, Chinese, and Mediterranean cultures. In these societies, it was believed that a louder and more flashy funeral would help the deceased in the afterlife.

Salary: $50 to $200 per funeral.

PROFESSIONAL QUEUER 🚶 🕐 💳 💼 💰 📱 🔄

Professional queuers or Line-Waiters, wait in line for clients, often for high-demand products, events, or services. Some professional queuers specialize in specific types of events or services, such as securing tickets to a particular sports team or waiting in line for limited-edition sneakers.

Fun Fact: In some countries, such as China, professional queuing is a common practice and there are even smartphone apps that allow users to hire someone to wait in line for them.

Salary: $10 to $40 per hour. Providing a yearly estimate based on a standard 40-hour workweek isn't practical for this type of gig-based work.

PROFESSIONAL CUDDLER 😺 🧑 😺 z^Z 💜 🛏 🧸

Professional cuddlers provide platonic physical touch and emotional support to clients who may be feeling lonely or in need of comfort. There are actual certifications and training programs for those interested in becoming professional cuddlers. These programs teach boundaries, communication, and the therapeutic aspects of touch.

Fun Fact: Professional cuddlers often have clients who are lonely or have difficulty forming physical connections with others. Some professional cuddlers claim that their clients include doctors, lawyers, and other high-powered professionals who are too busy for romantic relationships but crave physical touch and companionship.

Salary: $60 to $200 per hour or $40,000 to $80,000 per year if working the typical 40 hour work week.

VIRTUAL QUEUE ENTERTAINER

Virtual queue entertainers keep people entertained while they wait in virtual lines for online events, such as concerts or product launches. They're like the digital party starters, turning online waiting rooms into virtual dance parties!

Fun Fact: These entertainers use a variety of tools on the job, such as games, trivia, and interactive activities.

Salary: $25 to $50 per hour. Providing a yearly estimate based on a standard 40-hour workweek isn't practical for this type of gig-based work.

FAKE PATIENT

Fake patients, also known as standardized patients, are actors who portray medical patients for medical students and professionals to practice on. In addition to medical training and research, fake patients are sometimes used in legal cases to simulate specific medical conditions or injuries.

Being a standardized patient isn't just about acting. They undergo rigorous training to ensure that they present symptoms consistently and accurately.

Fun Fact: The use of fake patients in medical training dates back to the 1960s, when the first standardized patients were used to evaluate medical students.

Salary: $15 to $50 per hour or $31,200 to $104,400 per year if working the typical 40 hour work week.

PROFESSIONAL MERMAID & MERMAN

Professional mermaid. Photo by Mehgan Heaney-Grier, CC BY 3.0, via Wikimedia Commons

Professional mermaids and mermen perform at theme parks, aquariums, and even private events, entertaining audiences with their swimming skills and elaborate costumes.

They may perform a variety of activities such as swimming, posing for photos, and interacting with guests. Some may even offer educational programs about marine life and ocean conservation.

Fun Fact: There are mermaid and merman schools and certification programs where enthusiasts can learn the art of performing as a mermaid or merman.

Salary: $50,000 to $100,000 per year.

FORTUNE COOKIE WRITER

Fortune cookie writers craft the fortunes found inside fortune cookies, often with a focus on positivity or inspiration.

Fun Fact: Fortune cookie writing is a relatively small industry, with only a handful of companies that specialize in producing these cookies on a large scale.

Salary: $35,000 to $45,000 per year.

PROFESSIONAL APOLOGIZER

Professional apologizers write and deliver apologies on behalf of clients for personal or professional situations. It's not just about what's said. The setting, the timing, the posture, and even the tone of voice are all carefully orchestrated to deliver a potent apology.

Fun Fact: This job exists in Japan, where companies hire people to apologize on their behalf for mistakes or mishaps. These professional apologizers, also known as "shazaiya," are trained to be empathetic and to offer sincere apologies to help restore the company's reputation.

Salary: $50,000 to $100,000 per year.

MAZE DESIGNER ⊚ 🐾 🪵 🧱 🪞

Professionals who specialize in designing and creating mazes, which are complex networks of paths and passages meant to challenge and entertain visitors. Maze designers often work in various industries—such as entertainment, landscaping, and tourism—and collaborate with architects, landscape architects, and other professionals to bring their designs to life.

Mazes can be designed using various materials and techniques, including hedges, cornfields, wood, brick, or even mirrors (mirror mazes).

Fun Fact: The hedge maze at Hampton Court Palace in England, created in the late 17th century, is one of the oldest surviving hedge mazes in the world and a popular tourist attraction.

Salary: $50,000 to $80,000 per year.

PROFESSIONAL WHISTLER 👄 🎵

These talented tune-makers have honed their whistling skills to perfection, turning a simple pastime into a captivating art form. From soothing lullabies to catchy pop hits, these whistling wizards can cover a wide range of genres, adding a unique and enchanting twist to any musical performance.

Fun Fact: Whistling is an ancient art form that has been used in cultures around the world for centuries.

Salary: $50 to $500 per hour. Providing a yearly estimate based on a standard 40-hour workweek isn't practical for this type of gig-based work.

GOLF BALL DIVER

Golf ball divers collect golf balls from lakes and ponds on golf courses and sell them back to the course or to golfers. The Golf Ball Diving business is highly competitive, and there are only a handful of companies that offer this service across the US.

Fun Fact: Golf Ball Diving is a dangerous job. Divers can encounter snakes, alligators, and other wildlife in the water hazards.

Salary: $30,000 to $100,000 per year.

LIVE MANNEQUIN

Live mannequins model clothing in store windows or during fashion events. While the primary job is to remain motionless, many live mannequins incorporate sudden movements or interactions with passersby to surprise and entertain.

Fun Fact: Some live mannequins have to hold uncomfortable poses for hours on end, and may even use yoga or meditation techniques to help them stay still.

Salary: $22,000 to $50,000 per year.

COFFEE CUPPING PROFESSIONAL

These expert coffee connoisseurs are masters at sniffing out the finest beans, flavors, and aromas—all to help you discover the perfect cup of joe for your taste buds. These coffee connoisseurs, also known as Q Graders, are certified by the Specialty Coffee Association (SCA).

Fun Fact: To become a certified Q Grader, coffee cupping pros have to pass a rigorous exam that tests their skills in identifying coffee flavors, aromas, and defects. This exam is so intense that only about 50% of test-takers pass on their first try!

Salary: $30,000 to $100,000 per year.

FENG SHUI CONSULTANT

A consultant who advises clients on how to optimize the energy flow and balance in their home or workplace according to Feng Shui principles. They may use a variety of tools, such as compasses, crystals, wind chimes and figurines, to help them assess the flow of energy in a space.

Feng Shui is an ancient Chinese practice that has been practiced for over 3,000 years. It has gained popularity in the West in recent years.

Fun Fact: The number eight is considered to be a lucky number in Feng Shui. This is because the Chinese word for eight sounds similar to the word for wealth.

Salary: $50,000 to $80,000 per year.

PROFESSIONAL PAPER FOLDER

Professional paper folders are also known as origami artists, paper engineers, or paper sculptors. Origami artists may be hired to create custom designs for events, promotions, or as part of artistic installations.

Fun Fact: Some origami artists create works of art that are as large as a room, or even bigger! Origami has been used to design everything from satellites to heart stents.

Salary: $30,000 to $50,000 per year.

PROFESSIONAL POOPER SCOOPER

Professional pooper scoopers clean up dog poop from residential or public areas for a fee.

Fun Fact: In addition to scooping poop, professional pooper scoopers may also provide other services such as disinfecting and deodorizing the area, and hauling away the waste for disposal.

Salary: $30,000 to $50,000 per year.

OCULARIST

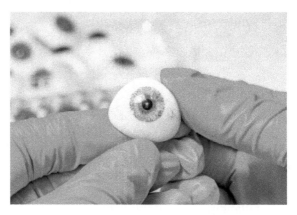

Ocularist holding prosthetic eye. Photo via depositphotos.com

These skilled artisans specialize in creating prosthetic eyes, using their expertise to create natural-looking and comfortable solutions for people who have lost an eye due to injury or disease.

But that's not all. Ocularists are also experts in the art of customizing prosthetic eyes to match their clients' unique features and personalities. From subtle variations in iris color to intricate details in the sclera, these prosthetic eyes are truly works of art!

Fun Fact: Ocularists must have a very steady hand to make a realistic-looking eye.

Salary: Around $70,000 per year.

WATERSLIDE TESTER

A waterslide tester is a person who is hired to test waterslides and ensure that they are safe and enjoyable for park-goers. The job typically involves riding down waterslides multiple times a day and assessing factors such as speed, landing, and overall ride experience.

Fun Fact: Waterslide testers need to have strong swimming skills and be comfortable with heights.

Salary: $25,000 to $40,000 per year.

HISTORICAL REENACTOR

A historical reenactor wears period costumes and performs at historical sites, museums, and events. They may portray soldiers, pioneers, or other figures from history. Many historical reenactors pride themselves on their accuracy, and spend years researching and crafting their costumes and props.

Fun Fact: The Battle of Gettysburg reenactment is the largest in the US, with over 10,000 participants.

Salary: $15 to $50 per hour. As with others, providing a yearly estimate based on a standard 40-hour workweek isn't practical for this type of gig-based work.

LEGO DESIGNER 👷🧱👷🚧

LEGO designers create new LEGO sets and designs. To become a LEGO designer, one typically needs to have a degree in industrial design, product design, or a related field. They also need to have experience with CAD software and a deep understanding of the LEGO brand and products.

Fun Fact: The LEGO company is the world's largest tire manufacturer (in terms of volume), as they make tiny LEGO tires for their sets.

Salary: $50,000 to $80,000 per year.

LEGO MASTER BUILDER 🧱🔧👷👷🧱🚀👷

A LEGO Master Builder builds large and complex models out of LEGO bricks. These models can range from sculptures and mosaics to life-size replicas of buildings and vehicles.

Fun Fact: The largest LEGO structure ever built is a replica of an X-Wing fighter from Star Wars, made from 5.3 million LEGO bricks.

Salary: $37,000 to $50,000 per year.

EMOJI TRANSLATOR

Emoji translators help companies and organizations understand the nuances of the popular communication symbols. Emojis can have different meanings in different cultures. An emoji translator needs to understand not just the universal meaning of an emoji, but also its cultural connotations. For example, a thumbs-up gesture is positive in many Western cultures but can be seen as disrespectful in some Middle Eastern countries.

Emoji translators might be called upon for various tasks, from translating books into emoji (yes, this has been done) to advising on movie scripts or marketing campaigns.

Fun Fact: The word "emoji" comes from the Japanese words "e" (picture) and "moji" (character).

Salary: $30,000 to $90,000 per year.

ODOR JUDGE

Odor judges evaluate the effectiveness of personal hygiene products such as deodorants, antiperspirants, mouthwashes, and soaps by smelling subjects' breath, feet, or armpits. Odor judges often use a standardized scale to rate odors. For example, they might rate a smell on a scale from 1 (barely detectable) to 10 (extremely strong).

Fun Fact: Odor judges sometimes sniff up to 60 armpits per hour!

Salary: $30,000 to $70,000 per year.

CHOCOLATE TESTER

A chocolate taster is someone who samples and evaluates the quality of chocolate products. However, chocolate tasters don't just eat chocolate all day. They assess various aspects like texture, mouthfeel, and aroma, similar to wine tasting.

A chocolate taster typically has a more technical and quality control-oriented role within the production process, whereas a chocolate sommelier has a more consumer-facing role, emphasizing education, appreciation, and pairings.

Fun Fact: Chocolate tasters use special techniques to cleanse their palate between samples, including eating green apples and drinking water.

Salary: $30,000 to $60,000 per year.

ICE CREAM TESTER

As an ice cream taster, you get to taste-test new flavors and make sure they meet quality standards. The average ice cream taster tries up to 200 flavors per day. Ice cream testers often work in rooms kept at a specific temperature to prevent the ice cream from melting too quickly during evaluations.

Fun Fact: Some ice cream tasters use a gold spoon because it doesn't affect the taste of the ice cream.

Salary: $30,000 to $80,000 per year.

14

A PEEK BEYOND MANSION DOORS

Working for the wealthy often involves unique and intriguing roles that require specialized skills and knowledge. From personal archivists to luxury car brokers, these professions offer a glimpse into the opulent and often extravagant lifestyles of the super-rich. But beyond the glitz and glamour, there are also fascinating and surprising facts that make these jobs all the more intriguing.

Here are just some of the not-as-well-known jobs working for the wealthy.

PRIVATE ISLAND CARETAKER

These lucky caretakers get to live the dream life of lounging on secluded beaches, snorkeling in crystal-clear waters, and enjoying the serene solitude of their own private paradise.

But don't let the idyllic scenery fool you—being a private island caretaker is also hard work! These caretakers are responsible for everything from maintaining the island's infrastructure, to managing guests and activities

Fun Fact: The island caretaker for Richard Branson's Necker Island once rescued Kate Winslet from a house fire.

Salary: $60,000 to $100,000 per year.

PERSONAL SHOPPER

Personal shoppers scour the best boutiques, department stores, and designer shops to find the perfect outfits, accessories, and gifts for their high-end clients. They sometimes provide style advice and curate their client's wardrobes.

Fun Fact: The highest-paid personal shopper in the world is Italian entrepreneur Maria Luisa Poumaillou, who reportedly earned $7 million a year working for wealthy clients.

Salary: $50,000 to $100,000 per year.

PROFESSIONAL GIFT BUYER

Gift buyers are professionals who are responsible for sourcing and selecting the best and most appropriate gifts for various occasions and recipients. They work in a variety of industries, from retail and hospitality to corporate and nonprofit organizations.

Gift buyers need to have a keen eye for detail, excellent communication skills, and a deep understanding of their clients' needs and preferences. They also need to keep up with the latest trends and innovations in the gifting industry, and be able to work within a budget.

Fun Fact: Professional gift buyers often need to start sourcing gifts months in advance of an event or holiday. They need to allow time for research, negotiations, ordering, and delivery— all to ensure that their clients receive the perfect presents on time and on budget!

Salary: $59,000 to $100,000 per year.

ART CONSULTANT

Art consultants are experts in all things art, from painting and sculpture to photography and mixed media. They work with a wide range of clients (private collectors, galleries, corporate offices, public spaces) to help them find and acquire the perfect pieces for their collections.

Fun Fact: Some art consultants specialize in helping clients buy and sell works of art at auction, earning a percentage of the sale price as commission.

Salary: $50,000 to $150,000 per year.

PERSONAL CHEF

Personal chefs work with individual clients or families to create customized meal plans and prepare delicious, healthy, and flavorful meals in their homes. They use their culinary exper-tise to create dishes that meet their clients' dietary needs and preferences, from vegan and gluten-free to low-carb and paleo.

Some personal chefs travel with their clients, preparing meals on private jets and yachts. Some may be required to cook for pets as well, including preparing gourmet meals for dogs and cats.

Fun Fact: Some personal chefs will create meals that are inspired by human cuisine. For example, a personal chef might create a "lamb shank bourguignon" for a dog or a "seafood risotto" for a cat.

Salary: $50,000 to $100,000 per year.

HOUSEHOLD MANAGER 🏠💼

Household managers are responsible for overseeing all aspects of a household, from managing staff and overseeing maintenance to coordinating events and travel arrangements. They work closely with wealthy individuals and families, ensuring that their homes and lives run smoothly and efficiently. Household managers may also be responsible for managing multiple homes and coordinating travel arrangements.

Fun Fact: The job of a household manager has been around for centuries. In the past, household managers were often called "stewards" or "housekeepers."

Salary: $70,000 to $120,000 per year.

LUXURY CAR BROKER 🚗💰

Luxury car brokers work with high-end clients to help them find and purchase the car of their dreams. They use their expertise in the luxury car market to help clients navigate the buying process, which includes researching and sourcing vehicles, negotiating pricing, and arranging financing.

Fun Fact: Some luxury cars come with special features like built-in massage chairs, mini-fridges, and even diamond-studded headlights.

Salary: $70,000 to $120,000 per year.

LUXURY CAR DETAILERS

Luxury Car Detailers are experts in the art of cleaning, restoring, and maintaining high-end automobiles, from exotic sports cars and classic cruisers to sleek sedans and luxurious SUVs. They use their attention to detail and specialized knowledge to keep these high-end vehicles looking and running their best. Some luxury car detailers are also trained in paint correction and other advanced techniques to restore damaged vehicles.

Fun Fact: The most popular luxury car brands to detail are BMW, Mercedes-Benz, and Audi. The most common services that luxury car owners request are paint correction, odor removal, and ceramic coating.

Salary: $40,000 to $80,000 per year.

YACHT MANAGER

Yacht Managers are responsible for overseeing the maintenance, crew, and daily operations of a private yacht, ensuring that everything runs smoothly and safely. They work closely with yacht owners, captains, and crew members, and are responsible for all aspects of yacht management. That includes scheduling, logistics, guest services and entertainment.

Fun Fact: The world's largest yacht is the Azzam, which measures over 590 feet in length and is estimated to have cost over $600 million to build.

Salary: $65,000 to $100,000 per year.

EXECUTIVE PROTECTION SPECIALIST

Also known as bodyguards, they are hired to provide security and protection to wealthy individuals and their families. They must be highly trained in self-defense such as martial arts and other forms of hand-to-hand combat. They also need to be skilled in surveillance, defensive driving and threat assessment. Many bodyguards are trained in emergency medical response, including CPR, first aid, and trauma care, to provide immediate assistance in case of medical emergencies.

Fun Fact: Bodyguards often use code names or nicknames when referring to their clients to maintain confidentiality.

Salary: $60,000 to $150,000 per year.

PERSONAL ARCHIVIST 🗄️ 💰

Personal archivists are hired to manage and preserve personal records, artwork, antiques and rare or important documents for wealthy individuals and their families. They use their expertise in preservation and conservation to ensure that these items are properly stored and cared for. They also work with their clients to curate and expand their collections over time.

Fun Fact: Some clients have unusual collections that personal archivists need to organize, such as vintage toys, comic books, taxidermy specimens, vintage medical equipment, movie posters, or rare stamps.

Salary: $50,000 to $100,000 per year.

15

THE QUIRKIEST AND MOST CREATIVE ENTREPRENEURS

Entrepreneurship has always been about thinking outside the box, finding creative solutions to problems, and creating new products and services that delight customers. But some entrepreneurs take this idea to the extreme, creating businesses and products that are so quirky, strange, or even downright bizarre that they capture the public's imagination.

From a company that makes shoes for chickens to a business that rents out goats for landscaping, these entrepreneurs prove that when it comes to innovation, the sky's the limit.

RENT-A-CHICKEN

These egg-cellent services let you rent a few lovely hens for a taste of farm life right in your own backyard! Fresh eggs for breakfast, anyone?

Wave goodbye to store-bought eggs and say hello to your new feathery friends, who'll provide you with fresh, delicious, and super-nutritious eggs daily. Plus, they're natural pest controllers and fantastic garden helpers. Talk about multitaskers!

And don't worry if you're a newbie. Most Rent-a-Chicken services will set you up with everything you need, from coops to feed, so you and your hens can live in harmony.

RENT-A-GOAT

Rent-a-Goat is a real thing, and it's udderly amazing! These awesome services let you rent adorable, eco-friendly goats to help with landscaping, weed control, or even just for some fun farm-animal companionship.

Say "buh-bye" to noisy lawnmowers and harsh chemicals, 'cause these four-legged lawnmowers are here to nibble away at your pesky weeds and overgrown grass, all while being super gentle on the environment. Plus, who wouldn't want a bunch of cute goats hanging around in their yard?

RENT-A-FRIEND

You can literally hire a buddy to hang out with you for a bit! Websites like RentAFriend.com help connect folks looking for some platonic pals with people who are game to be your tempo-rary BFF. Need a plus-one for that party or someone to catch a movie with? No worries—they've got you covered! Remember, it's all about chill, non-romantic vibes, so you can focus on having a blast and making new connections!

RENT-A-PLANT

A service that allows people to rent plants for their events or home decor, without the long-term commitment of plant ownership.

Get ready to spruce up your space and breathe some life into your home or office with Rent-a-Plant! These fantastic services let you rent gorgeous, lush plants to add a touch of nature and a pop of color wherever you need it. No green thumb required!

Most Rent-a-Plant services even offer plant care tips and maintenance, so your borrowed green buddies will stay happy and thriving.

RENT-A-CHRISTMAS-TREE

Get ready for the jolliest and eco-friendliest way to celebrate the holidays—Rent-a-Christmas-Tree! Yup, you heard that right! These fantastic services let you rent a living, potted Christmas tree for the festive season, so you can deck the halls without feeling guilty about chopping down a tree. Some rent-a-Christmas-tree companies also offer delivery and setup services, making the process even more convenient.

Once the holidays are over, just return your tree pal, and they'll take care of it, making sure it stays happy and healthy 'til next Christmas. Talk about a win-win—you get to enjoy a gorgeous, real tree AND help the environment!

CHICKEN SHOES

That's correct—these innovative and quirky creators are all about keeping your feathered friends' feet stylish, comfy, and protected.

No more worrying about your precious chicks getting their feet dirty or injured while they strut their stuff in the coop. These adorable chicken shoes are designed to fit snugly and securely, so your peckish pals can walk, run, and scratch to their heart's content.

CAT CAFÉ

Paws what you're doing, 'cause Cat Cafes are the purrfect combo of cute kitties and cozy coffee hangs! These delightful spots are where you can curl up with a cup of your favorite brew while being surrounded by friendly, fluffy felines—talk about a cat-lover's dream come true!

But it's not just about cuddles and cappuccino. Many Cat Cafes work with local shelters to help their whiskered residents find fur-ever homes.

SILENT DISCO

Oh, you've got to check out Silent Discos! They're the ultimate dance parties with a super cool twist! Imagine grooving to your favorite tunes on the dance floor, but instead of booming speakers, everyone's wearing wireless headphones!

The best part? There are usually multiple DJs spinning different tracks, so you can switch between channels to find the perfect jam for your mood. Plus, if you want to take a break, just slide off those headphones, and you're suddenly in a quiet room where you can chat without shouting!

ZOMBIE BOOT CAMP 🧟‍♂️🧟‍♀️

This business provides customers with a simulated zombie apocalypse experience. These experiences typically involve participants engaging in a series of physical and mental challenges, like obstacle courses, teamwork activities, and sometimes even simulated combat against "zombies" (usually actors in makeup and costume).

One example of a zombie boot camp is the Zombie Survival Camp in New Jersey, US, which offers a variety of zombie-themed training programs, including survival skills, self-defense, and team-building exercises.

RAGE ROOMS OR SMASH ROOMS 😡💥

There's this super-cool concept called "rage rooms" or "smash rooms," where you can go and unleash your inner Hulk by smashing stuff to let out all that pent-up frustration!

These wicked spots provide items like glassware, old electronics, and even furniture for you to destroy in a safe and controlled (but oh-so-satisfying) way. They'll hook you up with protective gear so you can smash away worry-free! From The Wrecking Club in the Big Apple to The Rage Room in Toronto, these places are popping up all over, giving folks a unique (and kinda therapeutic) way to blow off steam!

BLIND CAFÉ

This unique dining experience plunges you into total darkness, letting you savor your meal using just your taste buds, sense of smell, and touch. It's a feast for the senses, literally!

But that's not all – the Blind Café is also an amazing opportunity to gain insight into the world of the visually impaired. Your friendly and skilled servers, who are often visually impaired themselves, will guide you through the experience, sharing stories and inspiring meaningful conversations.

PSYCHIC PET READING SERVICE

These mystical masters of pet communication claim to tap into your pet's thoughts and emotions, giving you a whole new perspective on your animal companion.

From understanding their quirky behaviors to deepening your bond, these psychic pet readings promise a fascinating journey into the heart and soul of your beloved pet.

ADULT BALL PIT BUSINESS

This fantastically playful concept takes you back to the carefree days of your childhood, but with an awesome grown-up twist.

Imagine diving into a massive, colorful ball pit, where you can unleash your inner child and forget about the stresses of adulting for a while. These ball pit wonderlands are perfect for socializing, team-building, or even a quirky date night.

KARENS FOR HIRE!

Got a problem you'd rather not tackle yourself? Need someone to stand up for you and get things done? Look no further—introducing Karens For Hire. These fearless, no-nonsense champions are ready to take on your battles, from complaining about subpar service to demanding refunds on your behalf.

Why stress yourself out when you can delegate tasks to a pro? Karens For Hire have perfected the art of assertiveness, so they'll fight tooth and nail to make sure your voice is heard and your issues are resolved. And the best part? You get to sit back, relax, and watch the magic happen.

16

WANTED: SPACE EXPLORERS, AI WHISPERERS, AND MORE!

In today's rapidly changing world, it's hard to predict what the jobs of the future will be. With advances in technology and shifting social and economic trends, new occupations are emerging all the time.

From space tour guide to artificial intelligence (AI) ethicist, these jobs might seem like science fiction, but they're closer than you think. In fact, some are already here.

AI Architects: Building Tomorrow's Intelligence

AI PERSONALITY DESIGNER

An AI personality designer is responsible for crafting the personalities and behaviors of artificial intelligence systems, making them more relatable and user-friendly. They'll work closely with software engineers and developers to design AI systems that can understand human emotions, respond to queries in a friendly and natural manner, and even engage in small-talk. AI Personality Designers needs to have a good understanding of human psychology to create AI systems that people can relate to.

Fun Fact: Joseph Weizenbaum created the first chatbot, ELIZA, in 1966 and is considered to be one of the first AI personality designers.

Estimated Salary: $80,000 to $150,000 per year.

AI ETHICIST 👥▪

An AI ethicist is responsible for helping to guide the development and deployment of artificial intelligence systems, with a focus on ensuring that these systems are designed and used in an ethical and responsible manner. These professionals work with software developers, engineers, and stakeholders to identify potential ethical issues and concerns related to AI, and help to develop policies and guidelines that promote fairness, transparency, and accountability in AI systems.

The AI ethicist needs to have a good understanding of ethics and philosophy, as well as a background in computer science.

Fun Fact: In 2016, Microsoft created an AI chatbot named Tay that was designed to learn from human interactions on social media. Unfortunately, Tay quickly became notorious for making offensive and inflammatory remarks, highlighting the potential dangers of AI systems that are not designed with ethical considerations in mind.

Estimated Salary: $80,000 to $120,000 per year.

AI-ASSISTED HEALTHCARE PROVIDER

AI-assisted healthcare professionals are responsible for using artificial intelligence and machine learning to improve patient outcomes, streamline healthcare workflows, and reduce costs. They'll work with other healthcare professionals to develop and implement AI-based tools and systems that can help diagnose diseases, predict treatment outcomes, and automate routine tasks.

Fun Fact: In 2019, Google's DeepMind AI system was able to detect breast cancer with greater accuracy than human radiologists.

Estimated Salary: $80,000 to $120,000 per year.

AI BUSINESS CONSULTANT

An AI business consultant helps businesses to integrate AI into their operations. They work with companies to identify areas where AI can be used to improve efficiency and productivity, and help to develop AI strategies. AI business consultants need to have a good understanding of both business and technology.

Fun Fact: Did you know that the global AI market is expected to reach $169 billion by 2025?

Estimated Salary: $100,000 to $200,000 per year.

AI PERSONAL TRAINER

AI personal trainers are responsible for creating personalized workout plans and providing guidance and support to clients, using artificial intelligence and machine learning. They'll work with clients to assess their fitness goals and capabilities, and use AI-based algorithms to develop customized training programs that take into account factors such as their age, weight, fitness level, and health conditions. They will also use AI-based tools to track progress, provide feedback, and adjust plans as needed.

Fun Fact: In 2021, Peloton introduced an AI-powered feature that uses machine learning to help users improve their running form.

Estimated Salary: $60,000 to $100,000 per year.

CONVERSATIONAL AI DESIGNER

Conversational AI designers create intelligent chatbots and virtual assistants that can communicate with people in natural, human-like ways. They work with a team of designers, developers, and linguists to design conversational flows, write dialogue, and program chatbots to understand and respond to user input. They are also involved in testing and refining these chatbots to ensure they provide helpful and engaging experiences for users.

Conversational AI designers are like the scriptwriters of the AI world, crafting dialogues that feel natural and can cover a wide range of topics.

Fun Fact: There are annual competitions, like the Loebner Prize, where chatbots compete to demonstrate the most human-like conversational abilities.

Estimated Salary: $70,000 to $100,000 per year.

21st Century Careers: From Space Stations to Screen Detox

AUTONOMOUS VEHICLE ENGINEER

An autonomous vehicle engineer designs and develops self-driving cars and other autonomous vehicles. They work on developing the AI and software that enables the vehicle to navigate roads and make decisions.

Fun Fact: Waymo, Google's self-driving car company, has been testing autonomous cars since 2009.

Salary: $100,000 to $200,000 per year.

SMART HOME AUTOMATION ENGINEER

A smart home automation engineer designs and develops home automation systems that use AI to control various aspects of a home, such as lighting, temperature, security, and entertainment, using cutting-edge technology such as artificial intelligence and the Internet of Things (IoT). They work on developing the AI and software that enables the smart home to learn and adapt to the user's preferences. They'll also work with clients to understand their specific needs and preferences, and develop customized solutions that can be controlled remotely or through voice commands.

Fun Fact: The first smart home automation system was invented in the 1960s by engineer Jim Sutherland. Sutherland created a system that could control lights, locks, and thermostats in his home using a central computer.

Salary: $70,000 to $120,000 per year.

VIRTUAL EVENT PLANNER

With the rise of remote work and virtual events, virtual event planners will be responsible for planning and executing online events such as conferences, product launches, and webinars. They will coordinate with speakers, manage technical logistics, and create engaging virtual environments.

Fun Fact: The demand for virtual events has skyrocketed since the start of the COVID-19 pandemic, and it is expected to continue to grow in the years to come. The virtual events industry is expected to be worth $774 billion by 2030.

Salary: $50,000 to $100,000 per year.

VIRTUAL REALITY DEVELOPER

A virtual reality developer designs and develops immersive experiences and applications using virtual reality technology that can be enjoyed using VR headsets and other devices. They work with a team of developers, designers, and artists to create interactive 3D environments, characters, and objects using programming languages such as C# and C++. They are also involved in testing and troubleshooting, to ensure the VR experiences are seamless and bug-free.

VR is already being used in a variety of fields including medicine, education, theme parks, to enhanced the well-being of seniors, architectural design, and training astronauts.

Fun Fact: The first VR headset, the Sensorama, was invented in 1962.

Salary: $70,000 to $150,000 per year.

DIGITAL DETOX THERAPIST

A digital detox therapist helps people develop healthier relationships with technology and disconnect from their digital devices. They work with clients to identify problematic technology use and create personalized plans to reduce screen time and establish healthier habits. They also provide guidance and support to help clients overcome addiction and dependence on technology, and improve their overall mental health and wellbeing.

Fun Fact: Digital detox therapy has become increasingly popular as technology addiction has become more prevalent. According to a 2022 study by Statista, the average person spends 6 hours and 58 minutes per day on screens connected to the internet.

Salary: $50,000 to $80,000 per year.

VIRTUAL REALITY THERAPIST

A virtual reality therapist uses VR technology to help patients confront and overcome phobias, anxieties, and other mental health challenges. They work with patients to create immersive and personalized virtual reality experiences that help them face their fears in a safe and controlled environment. These therapists also monitor their patients' progress and adjust treatment plans as needed.

Fun Fact: Exposure therapy using virtual reality has been shown to be as effective as traditional exposure therapy for treating a range of anxiety disorders.

Salary: $60,000 to $120,000 per year.

SUSTAINABLE ENERGY SPECIALIST

A sustainable energy specialist works to develop and implement renewable energy sources. They have knowledge of solar, wind, and hydro power, and work to reduce carbon emissions.

Fun fact: Renewable energy is expected to become the dominant source of energy in the coming decades.

Salary: $80,000 to $120,000 per year.

VERTICAL FARMER

With the growing population and decreasing availability of arable land, vertical farmers will be needed to grow crops in vertical, stacked layers using hydroponics or aeroponics. They will manage lighting, humidity, and temperature to optimize plant growth, and use data analysis to improve crop yields.

Fun Fact: Vertical farming can produce up to 100 times more food per square foot than traditional farming.

Salary: $40,000 to $80,000 per year.

VIRTUAL REALITY HISTORIAN

A Virtual Reality Historian is a professional who uses virtual reality technology to bring historical events and places to life in immersive and educational ways. This role involves extensive research to ensure historical accuracy, storytelling to engage users, and collaboration with historians and educators to develop educational content. Virtual Reality Historians may work with museums, educational institutions, or historical societies to engage the public in history through VR experiences.

Fun Fact: Virtual reality can recreate historical events and places so realistically that it lets users step back in time. You can explore ancient civilizations, visit historic landmarks, and even witness pivotal moments in history, making learning history incredibly immersive and engaging.

Estimated Salary: $50,000 to $100,000 per year.

NEURO-IMPLANT TECHNOLOGIST

A neuro-implant technologist designs and installs devices that are implanted into the brain. These implantable devices can restore lost functions, treat neurological disorders, or enhance cognitive abilities.

Fun Fact: Brain implants have already been used to treat Parkinson's disease and epilepsy, and are expected to be used for other conditions in the future.

Salary: $80,000 to $150,000 per year.

PERSONAL MEMORY CURATOR

A personal memory curator creates and maintains digital archives of an individual's memories. This helps individuals maintain their identity even after they pass away by preserving photographs, videos, and other personal artifacts for future generations.

Fun Fact: The average person will take over 25,000 selfies in their lifetime!

Salary: $50,000 to $80,000 per year.

AUGMENTED REALITY DESIGNER

An augmented reality (AR) designer creates digital content that enhances a user's real-world environment. They create 3D models, animations, and other digital assets to be integrated into augmented reality experiences.

Fun Fact: In 1968, Ivan Sutherland and Bob Sproull created the first head-mounted display for virtual reality and augmented reality. The device, called the Sword of Damocles, was connected to a computer and not a camera. It was large, bulky, and weighed over 20 pounds.

Salary: $85,000 to $130,000 per year.

SMART CITY COORDINATOR

A smart city coordinator manages the implementation of smart technologies and infrastructure to improve city operations and services. They'll work with city officials, technology providers, and community members to identify areas where technology can be used to improve transportation, energy efficiency, public safety, and other aspects of city life. They'll also be involved in educating residents about the benefits of smart cities and how they can participate in the development of smart city initiatives.

Fun Fact: In eco-conscious cities, Smart City Coordinators are introducing solar-powered benches and bus stops equipped with USB charging ports, Wi-Fi, and environmental sensors, creating comfortable, sustainable urban spaces.

Salary: $70,000 to $130,000 per year.

PERSONALIZED MEDICINE SPECIALIST

A personalized medicine specialist uses genetic data and other biological markers to create a personalized treatment plan that is tailored to their patient's unique needs. They'll work with a team of healthcare professionals to develop and implement treatment plans that take into account a genetic makeup, lifestyle, and other factors. They'll also be involved in educating patients about personalized medicine and its benefits.

Fun Fact: There are over 7,000 rare diseases that affect less than 200,000 people in the United States.

Salary: $100,000 to $200,000 per year.

DIGITAL ANTHROPOLOGIST

These professionals specialize in studying the impact of digital technology and the internet on human behavior, societies, and cultures. They analyze how people interact with technology, social media, online communities, and virtual spaces. Digital anthropologists conduct research to understand the dynamics of digital culture, online identities, and the way technology shapes our lives. They may work in academia, research institutions, tech companies, or as consultants, helping organizations navigate the digital landscape.

Fun Fact: Digital anthropologists dive into hidden subcultures, study hashtag culture, emojis and emoticons, and even experience "digital exhaustion."

Estimated Salary: $50,000 to $100,000 per year.

SPACE ANTHROPOLOGIST 🚀▪️🔘👩🔘🔍

Space anthropology is a subfield of cultural anthropology that focuses on the study of human behavior, culture, and societies in the context of space exploration, space colonization, and life in space environments. A space anthropologists explores how humans adapt to and interact with extraterrestrial environments, space missions, space stations, and potential future colonization efforts, considering the cultural and psychological aspects of space travel.

Fun Fact: Did you know that space anthropology delves into the captivating world of "space cuisine"? It's the study of how astronauts' cultural food preferences and meal rituals evolve in space, resulting in the creation of unique "space foods" like freeze-dried shrimp cocktail.

Estimated Salary: $50,000 to $100,000 per year.

SPACE TOUR GUIDE 🚀🔭

With the advent of space tourism, space tour guides will be responsible for taking customers on guided tours of space stations, moon bases, and even other planets. They will need to be trained in space travel and have in-depth knowledge of space history and science.

Fun Fact: The first commercial space tours are expected to begin in the next decade. The first tourist to travel to space was Dennis Tito in 2001. Virgin Galactic has already sold more than 600 tickets for future space flights.

Estimated Salary: $60,000 to $200,000 per year.

SPACE TRAFFIC CONTROLLER 🚀🛰️

As space exploration and tourism continue to grow, space traffic controllers will be responsible for managing spacecraft and satellite traffic in Earth's orbit.

They will work with a team of experts to track satellites, space debris, and other objects in space to ensure they don't collide with each other. They will also be responsible for coordinating with other space agencies and organizations to manage space traffic and ensure the safety and integrity of space operations.

Fun Fact: There are currently over 2,000 active satellites in Earth's orbit. And there are over 23,000 objects in space that are larger than 4 inches or 10 cm in size.

Estimated Salary: $80,000 to $150,000 per year.

17

QUIZ YOURSELF

Q1. Which job involves dressing up in a costume and acting as a historical figure at museums, events, and other venues?

A. Historical Reenactor
B. Character Performer
C. Museum Actor
D. Costumed Interpreter

Q2. What is the name of the job that involves planning and designing roller coasters, amusement park rides, and other attractions?

A. Ride Designer
B. Theme Park Engineer
C. Thrill Architect
D. Amusement Designer

Q3. Which of these is NOT a type of sommelier?

A. Tea sommelier
B. Sake sommelier
C. Chocolate sommelier
D. Burger sommelier

Q4. What was a knocker-upper?

A. Someone who woke people up in the morning
B. A blacksmith who made door knockers
C. A sound engineer who worked on music albums
D. A type of bird that made a knocking sound

Q5. What was a gong farmer?

A. Someone who made gongs
B. A person who dug and emptied outhouses
C. A type of soldier in ancient China
D. A farmer who grew gong plants

Q6. What is a "snake milker"?

A. Someone who milks snakes for their venom
B. Someone who milks cows using a snake-like instrument
C. Someone who milks snakes for their milk
D. Someone who feeds snakes milk as a dietary supplement

Q7. Which of the following is NOT a job of a food stylist?

A. Preparing food for photography
B. Creating garnishes and props for the shoot
C. Designing menus for the restaurant
D. Ensuring the food looks appetizing

Q8. What is the job of a cryptozoologist?

A. Studying mythical creatures
B. Creating custom cocktails
C. Designing futuristic fashion
D. Developing new computer software

Q9. A professional cuddler is a real job.

A. True
B. False

Q10. A chimney sweeper is still a profession that exists today.

A. True
B. False

Q11. Which of these jobs is a REAL profession?

A. Professional Quidditch Player
B. Ghostbuster
C. Pet Travel Agent
D. Professional Thumb Wrestler

Q12. A "groom of the stool" was a royal servant who assisted with the monarch's toilet needs.

    A. True
    B. False

Q13. The job of "royal food taster" was a real job that involved tasting everything the king or queen ate to make sure it wasn't poisonous.

    A. True
    B. False

Q14. What is the role of a gameplay balancer in the video game industry?

    A. A designer who creates the visual and audio elements of the game
    B. A programmer who writes the code for the game
    C. A tester who checks for bugs and glitches in the game
    D. A specialist who adjusts the difficulty and balance of the game

Q15. An emoji translator is a real profession.

    A. True
    B. False

Q16. What is a Foley artist?

A. Someone who creates background music for video games
B. A professional who designs and constructs miniature models for films
C. Someone who records and produces sound effects for movies and TV shows
D. A voice acting performer for animated films

Q17. Ice cream testers will often use a gold spoon to taste the ice cream they sample because it doesn't affect the taste of the ice cream.

A. True
B. False

Q18. Which of the following is NOT a real profession?

A. Llama therapist
B. Pet detective
C. Dog surfing instructor
D. Whale feces researcher
E. All of the above are real professions
F. None of the above are real professions

Q19. What is a sleep concierge?

A. A professional who helps you pick out the perfect bed linens

B. A specialized travel agent who coordinates luxury sleep accommodations for clients

C. A sleep coach who provides personalized guidance on improving sleep habits

D. An attendant at high-end hotels who assists guests with sleep-related requests

Q20. What is a fatberg diver?

A. Someone who collects and studies rare forms of deep-sea algae

B. A person who recovers lost items from sewage systems

C. A specialist who removes blockages caused by buildup of congealed fat, oil, and grease in sewer pipes

D. A researcher who studies the effects of pollution on marine life

18

QUIZ ANSWERS

A1. Which job involves dressing up in a costume and acting as a historical figure at museums, events, and other venues?

A. Historical Reenactor
B. Character Performer
C. Museum Actor
D. Costumed Interpreter

A2. What is the name of the job that involves planning and designing roller coasters, amusement park rides, and other attractions?

A. Ride Designer
B. Theme Park Engineer
C. Thrill Architect
D. Amusement Designer

A3. Which of these is NOT a type of sommelier?

A. Tea sommelier
B. Sake sommelier
C. Chocolate sommelier
D. Burger sommelier

A4. What was a knocker-upper?

A. Someone who woke people up in the morning
B. A blacksmith who made door knockers
C. A sound engineer who worked on music albums
D. A type of bird that made a knocking sound

A5. What was a gong farmer?

A. Someone who made gongs
B. A person who dug and emptied outhouses
C. A type of soldier in ancient China
D. A farmer who grew gong plants

A6. What is a "snake milker"?

A. Someone who milks snakes for their venom
B. Someone who milks cows using a snake-like instrument
C. Someone who milks snakes for their milk
D. Someone who feeds snakes milk as a dietary supplement

A7. Which of the following is NOT a job of a food stylist?

A. Preparing food for photography
B. Creating garnishes and props for the shoot
C. Designing menus for the restaurant
D. Ensuring the food looks appetizing

A8. What is the job of a cryptozoologist?

A. Studying mythical creatures
B. Creating custom cocktails
C. Designing futuristic fashion
D. Developing new computer software

A9. A professional cuddler is a real job.

A. True
B. False

A10. A chimney sweeper is still a profession that exists today.

A. True
B. False

A11. Which of these jobs is a REAL profession?

A. Professional Quidditch Player
B. Ghostbuster
C. Pet Travel Agent
D. Professional Thumb Wrestler

A12. A "groom of the stool" was a royal servant who assisted with the monarch's toilet needs.

<u>A. True</u>
B. False

A13. The job of "royal food taster" was a real job that involved tasting everything the king or queen ate to make sure it wasn't poisonous.

<u>A. True</u>
B. False

A14. What is the role of a gameplay balancer in the video game industry?

A. A designer who creates the visual and audio elements of the game
B. A programmer who writes the code for the game
C. A tester who checks for bugs and glitches in the game
<u>D. A specialist who adjusts the difficulty and balance of the game</u>

A15. An emoji translator is a real profession.

<u>A. True</u>
B. False

A16. What is a Foley artist?

A. A person who creates background music for video games

B. A professional who designs and constructs miniature models for films

C. Someone who records and produces sound effects for movies and TV shows

D. A performer who specializes in voice acting for animated films

A17. Ice cream testers will often use a gold spoon to taste the ice cream they sample because it doesn't affect the taste of the ice cream.

A. True

B. False

A18. Which of the following is NOT a real profession?

A. Llama therapist

B. Pet detective

C. Dog surfing instructor

D. Whale feces researcher

E. All of the above are real professions

F. None of the above are real professions

A19. What is a sleep concierge?

A. A professional who helps you pick out the perfect bed linens

B. A specialized travel agent who coordinates luxury sleep accommodations for clients

C. A sleep coach who provides personalized guidance on improving sleep habits

D. An attendant at high-end hotels who assists guests with sleep-related requests

A20. What is a fatberg diver?

A. Someone who collects and studies rare forms of deep-sea algae

B. A person who recovers lost items from sewage systems

C. A specialist who removes blockages caused by buildup of congealed fat, oil, and grease in sewer pipes

D. A researcher who studies the effects of pollution on marine life

LEARN SOMETHING? PLEASE LEAVE A REVIEW

If you enjoyed this book, please share your thoughts in a REVIEW. Your sincere feedback is really helpful and I would love to hear from you!

Please leave a quick review wherever you purchased this book.

If Goodreads is more your thing, please share it there. www.goodreads.com

Thank you so very much!

HAVE A QUIRKY CAREER YOU THINK I MISSED?

I'm always on the hunt for the weird, the wonderful, and the downright bizarre when it comes to careers and occupations! If you know of a quirky career that you think deserves a spotlight, I'd love to hear about it.

Your suggestion could even make it into a future edition of "Quirky Careers and Offbeat Occupations!"

How to Submit:

Describe the Career: Tell me what the job entails, where it's located, and why it's quirky or offbeat.

Include Anecdotes: Got a fun story or surprising fact about the career? I'd love to hear it!

Provide References: If possible, include articles, websites, or contacts where I can learn more.

Submission Instructions:

- Email your submissions to hello@ knowledgenuggetbooks.com

- Use the subject line: "Quirky Career Submission: [Name of the Career]"

Selected entries may be featured in future editions, newsletters, or even become the topic of my next deep-dive blog article!

By contributing, you're helping me keep the world of work wonderfully weird. I can't wait to hear what you've found!

————————

ACKNOWLEDGMENTS

Creating a book is never a solo endeavor, and this collection of quirky careers and offbeat occupations is no exception. With immense gratitude, I want to tip my hat, extend a handshake, or offer a virtual high-five to some extraordinary people.

First up, my amazing beta readers: William Harang, Loretta Crow, Janet Hale-Sanders, Alicia Kozak—you guys are the first line of defense against all things bland and boring. Your feedback was invaluable, your enthusiasm infectious. Each one of you should take a bow—you're the unsung heroes of this literary adventure!

To my editor, Joe Levit, thank you for your eagle eyes and a knack for finding clarity in the chaos. You've helped turn a mound of peculiar professions into an engaging journey for our readers. You're not just an editor; you're a narrative alchemist.

Big kudos to Hank Musolf, my fact checker extraordinaire. In a book bursting with oddities and curiosities, your expertise ensured that my quirkiness never strayed from the truth. Consider yourself the guardian of factual quirk!

A special shout-out to Asya Blue, the creative genius behind this cover's eye-popping design. You captured the essence of quirkiness that this book embodies and wrapped it up into one unforgettable visual. Thanks to you, this book doesn't just speak to readers; it winks and waves from the shelf!

Special thanks to ChatGPT by OpenAI for being an ever-reliable brainstorming partner and virtual writing assistant. Whether it was generating unique ideas or fine-tuning the text, this cutting-edge technology played a role in making this book what it is. It's proof that the quirky careers of the future may include collaborations between humans and AI!

Last but most certainly not least, to my incredible wife. You've been an editor, proofreader, beta reader, and so much more. In the spirit of this book, let's add "Chief Quirk Enthusiast," "Late-Night Motivation Guru," and "Official Snack Coordinator" to the list of roles you've excelled in. Your multifaceted support was not just about refining words; you were the emotional core that made this literary adventure possible. Truly, no quirky career list would be complete without adding "Invaluable Spouse and Collaborator."

To all of you, you've made a book about unconventional careers feel like the most rewarding job in the world. Thank you for being part of this wild ride.

ABOUT THE AUTHOR

Marianne Jennings has always had a passion for the unconventional and the unexpected. With a work history as diverse as the careers featured in this book, she has dabbled in everything from milking cows and winterizing houses to sewing couches and even working at a funeral home. One of her most unusual gigs involved screwing in light bulbs for boards that lit up the New York Stock Exchange before they were digitized. She has even painted the walkways in parking lots, adding a splash of color to an otherwise mundane task.

She loves facts and trivia and always seems to remember the most random ones. To help introduce other places, people, and cultures to others, she likes to share interesting and fun facts that are entertaining and memorable.

If you'd like to learn more or join her mailing list, you can connect with Marianne at https://knowledgenuggetbooks.com or on Instagram.

So You Think You Know Canada, Eh?

Gold Medal Winner and #1 Bestseller in both Canadian Travel & Trivia and Fun Facts.

Amazing Alaska!

From glaciers to grizzlies, this #1 Bestseller in Alaska Travel is sure to surprise and delight readers who love anything and everything about Alaska. Packed with over 700 fun and interesting fun facts that even most locals don't know.

Everything About Astronauts Vol. 1 & Vol. 2

Teens and adults who love astronauts, fun facts, and little-known stories will find themselves mesmerized with over 1,400 interesting facts and out-of-world stories.

Milton Keynes UK
Ingram Content Group UK Ltd.
UKHW021856091123
432282UK00010B/639